DATE DUE

NOV 1 0 1994	DEC 0 8 1998
NOV 2 8 1994	MAR 0 9 1999
MAR 2 2 1995	APR 3 0 1999
April 5, 1995	JUL 0 1 1999
NOV 1 4 1995	NOV 0 1 2001
APR 1 0 1996	
NOV 1 2 1996	MAR 1 8 2003
OCT 2 1 1997	
NOV 0 5 1997	NOV 0 9 2010
NOV 2 5 1997	OCt. 25, 2017
DEC 1 7 1997	NOV 0 6 2017
FEB 2 7 1998	DEC 0 6 2017
OCT 2 7 1998	
NOV 2 4 1998	
DEC 0 8	

Straight Talk About Child Abuse

Straight Talk About Child Abuse

Susan Mufson, C.S.W., and Rachel Kranz

Facts On File
New York

Straight Talk About Child Abuse

Facts On File, Inc.
460 Park Avenue South
New York, NY 10016

Library of Congress Cataloging-in-Publication Data
Mufson, Susan.
 Straight talk about child abuse / Susan Mufson and Rachel Kranz.
  p. cm.
 Includes index.
 Summary: A guide for teens discussing the pervasive problem of child abuse in all forms, its effects, and possible solutions. A resource section provides lists of hotlines, associations, and agencies that offer assistance.
 ISBN 0-8160-2376-X
  1. Child abuse—United States—Juvenile literature. 2. Abused children—United States—Psychology—Juvenile literature.
 [1. Child abuse.] I. Kranz, Rachel. II. Title.
 HV6626.5.M84 1991
 362.7'6'0973—dc20   90-39758

A British CIP catalog record for this book is available from the British Library.

Facts On File books are available at special discounts when purchased in bulk quantities for businesses, associations, institutions or sales promotions. Please call our Special Sales Department in New York at 212/683-2244 (dial 800/322-8755 except in NY.

Text design by Catherine Hyman
Jacket design by Catherine Hyman
Composition by Facts On File, Inc.
Manufactured by the Maple-Vail Book Manufacturing Group
Printed in the United States of America

10 9 8 7 6 5 4 3

This book is printed on acid-free paper.

Contents

1

An All-Pervasive Problem

What Is Abuse?

Teenagers get a lot of messages telling them to trust adults. They're told that "father knows best," that they can always count on their family, that they should listen to their teachers. If they do question an adult's behavior, especially a family member's, they may get the message that they are being immature—or even disloyal.

Of course, ideally, teenagers *should* be able to trust adults. Most teens are dependent on their families for food and shelter, as well as for guidance and support. Teachers and other adult authorities are supposed to help young people learn and grow; their job is to understand what teenagers need and to help them develop the skills they need to get it.

But what happens when adults are *not* doing their job? What happens when a family member, a teacher, a relative, or a family friend acts destructively, rather than supportively? What about the father whose "discipline" turns into a violent beating, or the mother whose "constructive criticism" is actually a constant stream of insults? What about the family friend whose

1

friendly hug is starting to feel uncomfortable, or the relative who forces a teen into sexual contact and then blames the teenager for "coming on" to him or her?

This kind of behavior is known as *abuse*. There are many different definitions of abuse, but here's one that everyone can agree on: Abuse is what happens when an adult or another person of authority, such as a baby-sitter, takes advantage of his or her power over a child or a teenager. When this abuse takes the form of inflicting pain, it's called *physical abuse*, or *battering*. When it's in the form of insults, "mind games," or undermining a person's confidence, it's called *psychological* or *emotional abuse*. When it's in the form of unwanted sexual contact, it's called *sexual abuse*.

A Growing Awareness

For many years, most people believed that abuse of all types was relatively rare. The accepted belief was that a few misguided parents might beat their children, some "dirty old men" might approach little girls, but in general, most children were presumed to be safe.

Then in 1968, Dr. C. Henry Kempe and Dr. Ray E. Helfer published a book called *The Battered Child*. In it, they discussed the discoveries that Dr. Kempe had made while working with children at Colorado General Hospital. Like some other doctors before him, Dr. Kempe had begun to be suspicious of the many "accidents" that his young patients seemed to be having. The broken bones and bruises he was seeing just didn't seem to be properly explained by the children's parents. Dr. Kempe began to realize that the children were being beaten.

Even after *The Battered Child* was published, many people had a hard time accepting the extent of physical child abuse. Now, according to Margaret O. Hyde's *Cry Softly! The Story of Child Abuse*, we know that 2,000 to 5,000 U.S. children die each year as a result of attacks by their parents, guardians, or foster parents. Even though only 132,000 reports of sexual abuse were received by state agencies in the United States in 1986, the National Committee for Prevention of Child Abuse estimates that one million children are sexually abused each year and that 71 percent of all victims are girls. It is estimated that 1 million to 5 million children experience some kind of abuse each year, according to Hyde, and that each day up to 12 children are beaten severely enough to cause permanent brain damage. In fact, one study by the National Committee for Prevention of Child Abuse claims that every two minutes, a child is attacked by one or both parents.

As public awareness of this problem has grown, we've also learned about its devastating effects. The most dramatic of these, of course, is death. Tragically, very young children, particularly infants, are the most likely to be abused severely enough to die from it. Although kids from infancy through age 5 make up only about 28 percent of the child population (ages 0–18), a study of the federal government's National Center on Child Abuse and Neglect shows that they account for 74 percent of the deaths from physical abuse or neglect (when a child's physical needs are not being properly met).

Teenagers are even more likely than young children to be physically abused, since statistics show that abuse tends to increase as the children get older. We'll discuss this in more detail in the next chapter. Fortunately, however, while the physical abuse of teenagers is more frequent, it tends to be less severe than what infants experience. Some 40 percent of infant abuse is considered severe, as opposed to only 3 percent of teenager abuse.

Apart from the physical pain that is obviously suffered as a result of physical abuse, the psychological effects can be more protracted and devastating. According to the National Committee for Prevention of Child Abuse, some 97 percent of "hard-core" juvenile delinquents have a history of being abused, and some 80 percent of all prison inmates have such a history. This doesn't mean that a person who is being battered will inevitably end up in jail, but it does give us some indication of how serious and painful the effects of battering can be.

Psychological abuse on its own account can sometimes be as devastating. This type of abuse takes the form of behavior that undermines a person's self-esteem or self-confidence. Parents who are constantly telling a child that he or she is "no good," stupid, clumsy, or won't amount to much are engaging in psychological abuse. So are parents who expect their child to perform according to unreasonably high standards, or parents who expect their child to always consider the parent's needs before his own. Sometimes parents in this category may appear to be very loving and giving—but underneath the child receives the true message: Somehow, whatever he or she does, the parents will never really be satisfied.

Because psychological abuse doesn't involve a clear-cut physical action, there are far fewer chances to develop statistics about it. Margaret Hyde's *Cry Softly! The Story of Child Abuse* cites one estimate that, every year, there are close to a million incidents of this type of abuse.

Even though psychological abuse can't be easily measured, we do know quite a bit about its lifelong effects, which may include substance abuse, eating disorders, depression, difficulties with relationships and career, and even suicide.

If society took a long time to recognize physical abuse, it took even longer to recognize sexual abuse. Throughout the 1970s and 1980s, a number of books on child sexual abuse tried to bring this issue to public awareness. Nevertheless, when the *Los Angeles Times* published the results of its nationwide phone survey in 1985, many people were astonished by the results.

According to the *Times*, 22 percent of all the people living in the United States had been sexually abused before they reached the age of 18—that's 27 percent of the women in this country and 16 percent of the men. If the *Times* figures are accurate, that works out to 38 million adult survivors of childhood sexual abuse.

Furthermore, if sexual abuse is being practiced today at the same rate as when these adults were growing up, over 8 million girls and 5 million boys will be sexually abused before they reach the age of 18. This sexual abuse ranges from seeing an adult expose himself or herself to years of sexual intercourse between an adult and a child.

The *Times* figures may have surprised some people. But these statistics are only the latest in a series of studies that show just how widespread child sexual abuse has always been. In 1948, a famous study called the Kinsey report found that one woman in four reported some kind of childhood sexual abuse.

In 1979, sociologist Diana Russell did a random study of 900 San Francisco women. She found that 38 percent of them remembered being sexually abused by an adult relative, acquaintance, or stranger before they had reached the age of 18. In Russell's case, the 38 percent only included women who had actually been touched by their abusers. When she added in women who had had some kind of noncontact childhood experience—the figure went up to 54 percent.

Some people said that Russell's study wasn't accurate because it was limited to women in San Francisco. But when you put her study next to the Kinsey report and the *Times* survey, the results seem pretty clear. You can pretty much figure that of you and the people you know, one girl in four and one boy in six is facing some kind of sexual abuse, has already faced it, or is going to be facing it soon.

There are many different forms of sexual abuse. For a more complete definition of abuse, take a look at the beginning of chapter 2. For now, let's just say that sexual abuse is any kind of sexual contact between an adult and a person under 18, or between a teenager and a younger child, that the younger person feels uncomfortable about—looking, touching, playing, caressing, hugging, tickling, kissing, or talking dirty.

Myths and Facts About Abuse

Although physical, emotional, and sexual abuse are more visible to the public now than they ever have been, people still have many misconceptions about them. Here is a questionnaire about abuse that will allow you to test your ideas about this complicated topic. Try to take the test without looking at the answers. Then go on to read the answers and their explanations.

    1. Only strangers engage in sexual abuse.

    2. If people only beat their kids when they're drunk or high, then the alcohol or drugs is the real problem, and if that problem were solved, the abuse would stop.

    3. Some abusive parents love their children very much.

    4. The only people who sexually abuse boys are gay men.

    5. Physical, sexual, and emotional abuse are so common that you almost certainly know at least one person who is being abused in each way.

    6. Child abuse of all types is fairly recent problem.

    7. If a child enjoys sexual contact with an older person, it isn't really abuse.

    8. Any type of corporal punishment is actually physical abuse.

    9. If kids keep getting into trouble, they're at least partly responsible for their parents' anger and constant battering.

    10. Sexual abuse may take place even if there is no actual touching between the two people.

    11. Sexual and emotional abuse is found among all races, income levels, and types of families.

    12. Only uneducated people engage in physical abuse.

    13. If someone's parents seem to be constantly insulting or belittling their child, the child must have done something to provoke it.

_____ 14. The only reason that adults engage in sexual abuse is to get sexual pleasure.

_____ 15. A person who has been physically, emotionally, or sexually abused is ruined for life.

1. Only strangers engage in sexual abuse—False.

Anyone may be a sexual abuser. Baby-sitters, family friends, stepparents, teachers, employers, relatives, even fathers and mothers have been known to engage in sexual abuse. Likewise, anyone may be a target of sexual abuse. Both boys and girls, from infancy through age 18, have experienced abuse of this kind.

2. If people only beat their kids when they're drunk or high, then the alcohol or drugs is the real problem, and if that problem were solved, the abused would stop—False.

Alcohol by itself is never responsible for physical abuse. Neither is drugs. The parent who beats his or her children while under the influence has the same angry and violent impulses whether drunk or sober, high or straight. What the substances do often accomplish is to remove the inhibitions against acting on the impulses. In other words, a person doesn't beat a child because he or she is drunk. Rather, the person gets drunk to feel free to beat the child.

This means two things: One, it's very unlikely that a person who mixes alcohol or drugs with violent behavior is going to give up the alcohol or the drugs unless he or she is also ready to give up the battering. Without treatment for both the substance abuse and the physical abuse, it's unlikely that the person will be successful in giving up either one. Two, even if a physical abuser does manage to "go straight," he or she still has the same violent impulses as before, and without treatment will probably continue to act on them.

This is true of sexual abuse as well. Some sexual abusers only engage in abuse while drunk or high—but this doesn't mean the alcohol or drugs is responsible. It only means that the person "needs" the high to do what he or she wants to do anyway.

3. Some abusive parents love their children very much— True.

One of the difficult things for teenagers who are being abused to deal with may be their awareness of how much their parents love them. Parents who physically, emotionally, or sexually abuse their child may in fact love that child very much. Despite their love, however, they are compelled to act out their anger, frustration, or sexual impulses in ways that are harmful to their child.

Of course, a loving parent may cause just as much physical injury or emotional trauma as an unfeeling parent. Loving a child doesn't make the abuse hurt any less or remove its bad effects. What loving a child *may* do is give some parents the incentive to get treatment so that they can stop their abusive behavior.

4. The only people who sexually abuse boys are gay men—False.

Both women and straight men—that is, men who have no other homosexual relations—have been known to sexually abuse boys. Likewise, women who have no other homosexual relations have been known to sexually abuse girls.

5. Physical, sexual, and emotional abuse are so common that you almost certainly know at least one person who is being abused in each way—True.

Although we once believed that child abuse was extremely rare, we now know that it is quite common. However, because physical and sexual abuse is frequently hidden by children and their families, you may not be aware of it. With emotional abuse, you may be aware of how parents treat a friend of yours, but you may not have identified it as abuse.

6. Child abuse of all types is a fairly recent problem—False.

From ancient times until fairly recently, children were considered the property of their fathers, just as slaves were once considered the property of their masters. This meant that children were quite likely to be emotionally, sexually, and physically abused, as well as emotionally and physically neglected.

More recently, in 18th and 19th century America, many children worked long hours in mines, farms, and factories. Parents frequently abandoned children they could not afford to raise, which meant that roving gangs of children lived on the street, scavenging food and sleeping under bridges. Parents and employers were given the right to discipline children however they pleased, and children who were caught stealing might actually have been hanged for the offense.

Even in the earlier part of this century, many of these abuses were common. Likewise, sexual abuse of all types existed, and in view of the large numbers of abandoned children, may even have been more common than today.

Thus, what is new in our time is not child abuse, but *rather the idea that children have the right to be free of abuse*, as well as the social concern with this problem.

7. If a child enjoys sexual contact with an older person, it isn't really abuse—False.

Some children may find some pleasure in the sexual abuse that is forced on them. They may find this pleasure confusing, since they know that they didn't choose the sexual relationship. The sexual abuser may also tell the child that the pleasure is evidence that the child actually wanted the sexual relationship.

However, even if the child's body responds to the sexual abuse with pleasure, this doesn't mean that he or she is responsible for the abuse. The child may enjoy the attention, the cuddling, or other signs of physical affection without desiring a sexual relationship. It is an adult's responsibility to set sexual boundaries with children—children are *never* responsible for sexual abuse, no matter what feelings they have about it.

8. Any type of corporal punishment is actually physical abuse—Opinion.

We haven't answered True or False to this one, because there are many different opinions about it. Some people believe that it's abusive for adults to use *any* kind of physical force with children. They believe that such punishment is an unfair use of adult's superior physical strength and power, and that what the child learns from a spanking or a slap is that force should be used to settle an argument.

Other people believe that there's no real harm in an occasional spanking, provided that it's done within certain limits. If the parent is able to set limits on how much pain he or she causes, and if the child is old enough to understand the relationship between the punishment and the "crime," then it's possible that a spanking is not abusive, even though it may not be the most effective form of punishment.

Whatever your feelings on corporal punishment, however, you should be aware that battering and physical abuse may be disguised as routine punishment. A more detailed definition of what counts as physical abuse can be found at the beginning of chapter 2.

9. If kids keep getting into trouble, they're at least partly responsible for their parents' anger and consequent battering—False.

Just as a child is never responsible for sexual abuse, so are children never responsible for physical abuse. No matter how "badly" a child behaves, battering is never justified.

Sadly, one of the messages that abused children get is that they *are* responsible for their bad treatment. If a boy spills his milk and his father responds by slapping him, or by shaking him until he's dizzy, or by throwing a toaster at him, it seems reasonable to the child to assume that if he hadn't spilled the milk, his father wouldn't have hurt him. If a girl's mother promises to beat her with a strap every time she comes home late, and then does so, the girl may believe that her mother is only implementing a "reasonable" punishment.

Sometimes children do act badly. In fact, children sometimes act badly on purpose to get the parental attention that they can't get in any other way. Even if the child is deliberately acting badly, however, the child is *not* asking to be battered or abused. No matter how a child acts, adults have the responsibility to treat them decently.

10. Sexual abuse may take place even if there is no actual touching between the two people—True.

You can find a more complete definition of sexual abuse at the beginning of chapter 2. For now, let's just say that sexual abuse is any kind of sexual contact between an adult and a person under 18 or that between a younger child and a teenager toward whom the younger person feels uncomfortable. This kind of contact certainly may include touching the child, as well as talking dirty, spying on, or the older person's exposing himself or herself to the child. Both children and adults have a right to be free of such unwanted behavior. Because children are so dependent on adults, they have a special right to expect that adults and figures of authority will not abuse their power.

11. Sexual abuse and emotional abuse are found among all races, income levels, and types of families—True.

For many years, people believed that poor people were more likely to engage in sexual abuse. We now know this isn't true. What is true is that poor people are more likely to be observed by social workers, public health nurses, and doctors at public hospitals and clinics. Thus their problems are more likely to find their way into statistics. People with more money are more likely to avoid the social service system and to make use of private counselors and physicians. Thus their problems may be more easily hidden.

Likewise, for years the experts believed that less educated people were less likely to be good parents than people with more education. Again, we now understand that this isn't true. Even if a parent knows the latest child-rearing theories, he or she may still feel compelled to treat a child abusively—perhaps without even realizing it.

12. Only uneducated people engage in physical abuse—False.

Education doesn't guarantee being a good parent. Neither does money. There may be some evidence that physical abuse takes place somewhat more often in families that are suffering economic problems. On the other hand, as we just saw, it's also possible that the battering in these families is just more visible to the public health and social service systems. In any case, even if it turns out that there is somewhat more physical abuse among poor families, a significant amount of physical abuse takes place in every income and education category.

13. If someone's parents seem to be constantly insulting or belittling their child, the child must have done something to provoke it—False.

In this way, emotional abuse is like physical and sexual abuse: The child is never responsible for it. Parents don't emotionally abuse a child because the child deserves to be abused; parents emotionally abuse a child because the parents have some inner need to do so.

The problem, of course, is that children love and depend on their parents and want to please them. If parents seem to believe that their children are stupid, clumsy, or otherwise "difficult," children may try to make their parents seem correct by actually acting according to their parents' insults. This may be less painful and frightening than facing the truth: The parents are the ones who are acting badly, not the child.

14. The only reason adults engage in sexual abuse is to get sexual pleasure—False.

Some sexual abuse really isn't about sex. It's about power. Some adults or teens engage in sexual behavior with much younger people to enjoy their own sense of power over the other person. That power may take the form of forcing the person to perform sexual acts, or of pretending that the younger person is totally loving and devoted. For these abusers, engaging in sexual behavior with a person who is too young or too dependent to make that choice is a power game, not a sexual relationship.

Other abusers really do consider children a source of sexual pleasure. These people may feel powerless and insecure—perhaps because they, too, were sexually abused as children. Their sense of being powerless is so great, and so frightening to them, that they only feel comfortable with children. These abusers may experience their sexual relationship with children as both sexual and loving. This can be very confusing for the child, who may welcome the love but wish that it didn't come in a sexual form.

15. A person who has been physically, emotionally, or sexually abused is ruined for life—False.

It's true that any kind of abuse can have damaging effects, which will last until the abused person has worked them through. (For more about this process, see chapter 3.) But it's also true that some people do work through the effects of their abuse and go on to have satisfying work lives and family lives as adults.

The Many Faces of Abuse

Here are some stories of different kinds of teenagers and their experiences. These stories are *composite case histories;* that is, they represent a combination of many different real-life stories.

These stories are very different, but they all have one thing in common. Each of these teens is being affected by abuse or neglect. As you will see, neglect can be physical—as when a child is not given enough food or appropriate clothing. Neglect may also be emotional—as when a child is not given the love, attention, and educational resources that he or she needs.

Physical Abuse and Neglect

- Fourteen-year-old Geneva knows that her parents are usually proud of her. Sometimes, though, she makes mistakes. Once, she played the radio so loud that it woke Geneva's father up from his afternoon nap. Another time, she was 15 minutes late coming home. When these things happen, Geneva knows what to expect: Her father beats her with a strap, leaving big welts and, later, scars. Geneva tells herself that her father is only trying to teach her an important lesson. But somehow she knows that her friends aren't treated this way by their parents. Even though she's sure that her father is acting correctly, she does her best to hide the scars. If someone does see them, she makes up a story, like, "I fell down the stairs," so that no one will guess what her father has done. Geneva has always been shy. Lately, she finds that she doesn't really feel like talking to anyone.

- Lou is 16. His father left home when Lou and his two younger sisters were still babies. Ever since Lou can remember, his mother has had a terrible temper. When she gets mad, she just lashes out. Once she threw a frying pan full of sizzling bacon grease at Lou's sister and they had to take her to the emergency room. Another time she started beating Lou with a metal lamp. As soon as the beatings are over, Lou's mother cries and begs her children to forgive her. She buys them presents and makes them special treats, saying, "You know I love you, don't you?" Lou feels sorry for his mother, and he feels that he should be doing more to help her. Then maybe she wouldn't get mad and hurt them the way she does. Most of the time, Lou stays home and tries to keep her company. On weekend nights, though, he just has to cut loose. He goes out drinking with a bunch of guys and they do crazy things, like playing "chicken" in their cars.

- Even though Maria is only 13, she feels like she is the mother of her younger brothers and sisters. Her own mother has a drug problem and is hardly ever home. When she is around, she's not much help. This year things are worse than usual. Maria has no winter coat, and her only pair of school shoes are full of holes. Sometimes the only thing to eat in the house is cold cereal. Maria feels like she worries all the time about where to find money and how to take care of the other children. She hates her mother and is always angry with her. But Maria also feels that if she told anyone about her problems, she'd get her mother into trouble and bring shame on the family. So she continues to try to cope on her own.

Geneva, Lou, and Maria are all facing some form of physical abuse or neglect. In Geneva's case, the battering is disguised as a legitimate form of punishment. Geneva tells herself that her father isn't trying to hurt her—he loves her. He just wants to teach her a lesson. But she also suspects that she doesn't deserve to be beaten so severely, no matter what she has done. After all, none of her friends' fathers hurt them as badly has her father hurts her.

Geneva deals with her conflict by pretending that it doesn't exist. Even while she tells herself that her father is right, she tries to hide the truth about his actions, even from herself. Because Geneva is trying so hard not to tell the truth about her father, she has become very fearful of talking to anybody. Geneva may tell herself that she doesn't mind her father's actions—but they are affecting her life in ways that she's not even aware of.

Lou and Maria are very well aware that they have problems with their parents. But instead of holding their parents responsible for their actions, Lou and Maria try to take that responsibility for themselves. Lou would like to believe he can help his mother. It's less painful for him to believe that he *could* help than to accept the harsh reality that there's really nothing he can do for her. So Lou's buried anger and resentment come out in another way: in his reckless behavior with his friends. There he endangers the lives of others and of himself—just like his mother does.

Maria, too, would like to believe that she can take over the responsibilities of an adult. In fact, however hard she may try, a 13-year-old girl cannot possibly fulfill those responsibilities. She certainly can't earn the money needed to support a family, nor can she remedy the problem of physical neglect all by herself. But because Maria's mother has left these responsibilities to Maria, Maria honestly believes that it is her job to take care of her family. Instead of admitting that she can't do this job, it seems easier to Maria to try to "grow up" and do it.

The price Maria pays for this decision is a big one. Because she really *can't* do what an adult does, she feels worried and insecure all the time. She feels as if she's constantly failing, as if she's proving to everyone what a worthless person she is. Because Maria doesn't have a realistic idea of what she should expect of herself, she thinks of herself as a failing adult, instead of as a successful 13-year-old.

Emotional Abuse and Neglect

- Jerry is 17 years old, but many people mistake him for much younger. His parents pick out all his clothes for him and they dress him in styles that seem more like what a grade-school kid would wear than like those of a high-school senior. Jerry's parents won't give him permission to have an after-school job, or even to go out for after-school activities because they say he "can't handle the responsibility." They are full of praise for his being "such a good boy," but they do like to tease him about being careless and forgetful. When he gets mad, they look surprised and say, "We were only teasing! Why are you so sensitive?"

- If you asked 16-year-old Elena about her family, she'd tell you they were fantastic. She and her parents live in a beautiful house and there always seems to be enough money to buy Elena anything she wants. Although her parents have some rules about curfews and chores, they're much less strict than most of her friends. Elena's parents are always telling her how much they love her and how proud they are of her. Yet somehow, Elena feels that something is missing, something isn't quite right. For example, when she goes to give her mother a hug, her mother always pushes her away, holding her at arm's length and saying, "You're so beautiful. I love you so much." Elena hears the words, but she doesn't *feel* loved—she feels that since her mother doesn't want to hug her, that her mother doesn't love her. These feelings make Elena feel very guilty. Since her parents are obviously so great, there must be something really wrong with her.

- Seth is 13 and he's hated his parents ever since he could remember. His father is always telling Seth that he is a wimp. When Seth does something well, his father laughs and says, "So now you think you're special?" When Seth does something wrong, his father gets furious and says, "Why can't you do even one thing right?" Seth's mother seems to be the opposite. When Seth does something well, she gets nervous and says, "Don't expect it to always be like this." But when Seth has problems, she makes a big fuss over Seth, telling that no matter what else happens, *she'll* always love him. Seth thinks his parents are both jerks, but he also thinks they're probably right: He's not so special, and even when he's having a happy time, he doesn't really expect it to last.

Jerry, Elena, and Seth are all facing emotional abuse or neglect. Their parents are treating them in ways that make it very difficult for these teenagers to grow up feeling confident of themselves and good about the world. Instead, their parents are teaching them that they are not equipped to handle life's problems, that they can't trust their own perceptions, and that they probably don't deserve to be happy.

Jerry's parents seem to care for him, but their behavior is emotionally abusive. Although Jerry is almost an adult, his parents insist that he act like a child. Of course, many teenagers feel that their parents should allow them more independence in their choice of dress, friends, and behavior. But Jerry's parents really have gone to an inappropriate extreme. With their words and actions, they are teaching Jerry that he's not capable of functioning as an adult, that he can only hope to be an obedient little boy, no matter how old he actually is. With messages like these, Jerry will have an extremely hard time going away to college or holding a job, where more adult behavior will be expected of him.

Elena has a different kind of problem, which we might call emotional neglect. Although it seems that her parents are kind to her, some real emotional bond is missing. Because there are no outward signs of this problem, Elena has come to doubt her own perceptions. Yet somehow, a person's feelings always come out. Elena has tried to bury her feeling that something is wrong with her parents' treatment of her—so now she feels that something is wrong with her treatment of them. Her price for not facing the truth about her parents is carrying around an enormous load of guilt.

On the surface, Seth is very well aware of his problems. He's critical of his parents and can describe to you quite specifically what he doesn't like about what they do. Yet Seth has absorbed more of their messages than he has realized. Even though he says he hates his parents, on some level, Seth also loves them and wishes that he could trust them. So he tries to turn them into trustworthy people by believing what they say—even though he says he doesn't. Until he can face all his complicated feelings about his parents, Seth may very well go on believing their version of reality and feeling bad about himself.

Sexual Abuse

- When Suzy was eight, her baby-sitter asked her to keep "a special secret" with him. He fondled her genitals and asked her to touch his penis. When he touched her, sometimes it felt good, but it also felt a little "yucky," and she felt funny about it. She told her parents that she didn't like the baby-sitter and they never hired him again. Now Suzy is 13 and starting to go out with boys. She finds that she feels very guilty and uncomfortable whenever a boy tries to put his arm around her or hold her hand, but she doesn't know why she's reacting the way she is.

- Carlene is 15. She gets good grades, gets along with students and teachers, and is on the cheerleading squad. She goes out with lots of guys, but it's never very serious. Everyone agrees that Carlene is smart, popular, and seems to have it made. What they don't know is that Carlene's stepfather has been having intercourse with her since she was 10. Carlene feels like she is constantly putting on an act, that she's really two people—the nice girl that everybody knows and the bad girl she feels like inside. She's afraid to have a boyfriend or a girlfriend because they might find out her secret and she'd get her family into trouble.

- Seventeen-year-old Marc has always gotten along all right with his parents. For a few years, though, he's noticed that his mother is finding excuses to come into his room and watch him get undressed. Sometimes she asks him for help hooking up her bra or buttoning up a dress when she isn't wearing anything underneath. When this happens, Marc gets an erection, and then he feels guilty. If he asks his mother for more privacy, she just laughs and says, "You haven't got anything I haven't seen before."

Suzy, Carlene, and Marc have all faced unwanted sexual contact with adults or older people whom they have known and trusted. In Suzy's case, the abuse has ended, but its bad effect have not. Suzy may feel guilty about having enjoyed the sexual contact with the babysitter. At the same time, she knows that she didn't really want to be sexually intimate with him at that young age. These confusing feelings are making it difficult for her to go on and decide what kind of sexual contact she does want, now that she is older.

Carlene and Marc have another kind of problem. They, like all children, want to believe that their families know best and have their best interests at heart. So what do they do if a family member seems to be acting abusively? How can they believe that a loved one is actually treating them very badly?

Carlene handles the situation by pretending it isn't happening. She goes along with her stepfather's demands, but she tries to pretend that she's another person while she's doing it. The price she pays for this is to feel as though she's constantly a phony. When she's at school, she's hiding the truth about her family life. When she's with her stepfather, she's hiding her angry and confused feelings about their relationship. She may be even more angry because part of her likes the love and attention that she seems to be getting. Carlene handles these confusing feelings by trying not to have any feelings at all.

Marc handles the situation by going out with lots of girls at school. He needs to prove to himself that he's not a mama's boy, that he can be a real man, even if his mother seems to have extra power over him by awaking his sexual response. But because Marc doesn't trust his mother, he doesn't really trust the girls he goes out with, either. He thinks they might want to control him, like his mother seems to, and he worries about whether they like him for himself or just for his ability to be a good lover. Marc handles his confusing feelings by having lots of sexual relationships that never seem to last for very long or go very deep.

Recognizing Abuse

As you can see, physical, emotional, and sexual abuse may take many different forms. But they all have one thing in common: They all have powerful effects on the children and teenagers involved. Even if people try to pretend that such abuse doesn't really matter, that "I can take it," or "I really never think about it," in fact the abuse is shaping the way they feel about the world and themselves.

The good news is that if someone recognizes that abuse is going on and acts to stop it, it's possible to work through the bad effects and to go on to establish happier relationships. Sometimes, if the abuser is a family member, he or she may also get help, and the family may be able to come together on a new basis. Even if the abuser doesn't want to change, however, it's possible to stop the abuse, by leaving the home or having the abuser leave. And it's possible to get help and support for working through the effects of abuse—no one has to do that alone.

The first step toward stopping the abuse is to recognize it. If you suspect that you are being abused, or that you have been abused, go on to chapter 2, where we give more complete definitions of physical, emotional, and sexual abuse. But what if you're wondering whether anyone you know has been abused?

Unfortunately, emotional abuse is much more subtle than the other two kinds and is harder for an outsider to recognize or intervene in. Here are some common signs that may indicate sexual abuse, physical abuse, or physical neglect. Of course, any of these signs *could* be caused by something else, but they may lead you to look further:

Physical Abuse or Neglect

- Dirty clothing, body odor, unkempt appearance.
- Unexplained injuries, especially more than once.
- Burns or bruises, especially more than once.
- Arriving at school early and leaving late.
- Long sleeves in warm weather.
- Engages in violent behavior.
- Engages in dangerous behavior.
- Talks about beatings.
- Seems overly anxious and eager to cooperate.
- Seems secretive, withdrawn.
- Always searching for favors and help.

Sexual Abuse

- Sexual acting out—has lots of sexual partners, has partners who are much older or much younger.
- Sexual avoidance to an unusual extent, seems overly ashamed or uncomfortable about sexual relations or about "normal" activities such as undressing and showering in a gym class with members of the same sex.
- A sudden change in behavior: withdraws, loses interest in former activities, loss of concentration, change in personality or relationships, drop in grades.
- A sudden dislike of a particular person, activity, or place; not wanting to go somewhere or do something that was formerly a routine or pleasant activity.

The last two signs suggest that some kind of sexual abuse has recently taken place, creating the sudden change in behavior. The person may be blaming himself or herself for the abuse, or may be feeling suddenly powerless because he or she wasn't able to stop the abuse.

In addition, all kinds of abuse may be marked by poor grades, problems with drugs or alcohol, suicidal thoughts and actions, and eating disorders (compulsive eating and obesity; bulimia, eating and then forcing yourself to throw up; or anorexia, eating so little that you endanger your health). Likewise, all kinds of abuse may be marked by people being isolated, with no close friends or companions, an unwillingness to invite friends home or talk about parents, and a sense of depression and hopelessness about the future.

Using This Book

This book is your resource. If you or someone you know is being abused, you probably want to stop the abuse, but you may not know what to do. You may also be worried that you are wrong, that you are imagining a problem where none exists. Or, if you are certain that you or someone else is being abused, you may not know what is likely to happen if you do take action.

This book is designed to help you answer those questions, so that you can recognize abuse and take action to stop it. At the beginning of chapter 2, you'll find more complete definitions of each kind of abuse, as well as a discussion of who may be an abuser and why adults and teenagers engage in abuse. You'll also find more complete stories about the teenagers in this chapter, so that you can more easily recognize what abuse looks like and how it affects people.

Chapter 2 goes on to a more complete discussion of the ways in which abuse might affect someone, explaining how and why this experience can shape a person's life. Sometimes, it may seem that abuse only affects one area of life—the relationship with the abuser. But in almost all cases, abuse and its effects spill over into friendships, sexual relationships, school, and work, as well as into the way that the abused feel about themselves. It's important to recognize the deep and persistent effects of abuse, because that makes it very clear why the abuse must be stopped.

In chapter 3, you'll find a discussion of why people may choose *not* to ask for help in ending an abusive relationship. You may see yourself or someone you known in this discussion, so that you'll have more resources and information when it comes to making your decision. We'll also talk specifically about what you can do when you suspect that someone you know is being abused.

Chapter 3 will also talk about why it's important to stop abuse and get help for the abused person, what can happen if abuse is not stopped, and what becomes possible if it is. Finally, this chapter will describe what may happen once you or someone you know does decide to report the abuse.

Chapter 4 has more concrete information. It's a resource section, listing hotlines, national associations, and state agencies that offer various kinds of assistance to abused teens, abusers, families, and friends. Some of the resources there are anonymous—that is, you can use them without telling anyone your name. If you think that you or someone else is being abused and you're not ready to report the abuse to the authorities, you may wish to call a hotline and talk about your problem anonymously, with an expert. This person can give you an even better idea of what to expect if you do decide to report the abuse.

One of the most painful parts of abuse is that the person being abused is expected to keep it a secret. The abuser may threaten, lie, or play on the abused person's guilt to insure that the abuse is kept hidden. So breaking the silence about abuse can be scary, difficult, even painful. It can bring up all sorts of confusing feelings, which at this point may seem more frightening that the abuse itself.

But abuse is *never* the abused person's fault. And every person deserves to be free of it. Taking action to help yourself is your right—and it can make things better. Use this book as your resource to get the help you deserve.

2

The Nature and Effects of the Different Types of Abuse

Definitions of Abuse

The first step in stopping abuse is to recognize it. Sometimes this may be difficult. What is the line between a routine spanking and an abusive beating? How can you tell the difference between a painful fight with your parents and actual emotional abuse? What is the difference between ordinary, pleasurable physical affection and sexually abusive touching and kissing? If a person has grown up with a certain pattern of abuse, it may seem normal. Even if you recognize that other families act differently, your own family's behavior may not seem abusive, but merely "different."

There are many good reasons why a person would not want to recognize abuse. We'll talk more about them at the beginning of chapter 3. For now, let's just say that it's possible to love someone very much—and to recognize that nevertheless, he or she is abusing you. Such a recognition may be very painful, but ignoring the truth may be more painful. It may also help to realize that someone can act abusively while still loving the person that he or she is abusing.

As you read the following definitions, you may find yourself feeling relieved or excited. You may have the feeling that you're finally understanding something that has happened to you or to someone else, that you're not alone with this information any longer.

Or you might find yourself feeling anxious or angry. Perhaps that's because you see something in these definitions that you recognize. If you find yourself having these feelings, let yourself be aware of them. See if you can keep reading and learn something about why you're feeling that way. Pay attention to your feelings. If it's too difficult to keep reading, you may want to stop and come back to this book another day. But do come back and keep reading, even if you only read a little bit at a time.

Physical Abuse and Neglect

The U.S. Congress in the Family Service Act of 1988 came up with a definition of all types of abuse, which may help us to understand physical abuse and neglect. Here are the parts of Congress's definition that apply to physical abuse and neglect: "physical . . . injury . . . [or] negligent treatment or maltreatment of a child under the age of 18 by a person who is responsible for the child's welfare under circumstances which indicate that the child's health or welfare is harmed or threatened thereby."

What exactly does that mean? It means that any physical action or neglect that harms the health or welfare of someone under 18 is considered physical abuse or neglect—and, incidentally, is against the law. In other words, you have the right to expect that your parents, stepparents, guardians, foster parents, teachers, religious and spiritual leaders, and

legislature [handwritten margin note]

other adult caregivers will respect your health and welfare, and will not take advantage of their power and authority to harm you.

Now that we have the important words "health and welfare," we have a starting point for a definition of physical abuse. If a parent gives a toddler a few spanks on the rear, through the heavy padding of diapers and clothes, does this harm the child's health or welfare? Probably not—even though the child may not like it very much. But if a parent hits a toddler on a bare bottom hard enough to leave a bruise, this has harmed the child's health. There's a bruise—and there's the harm to the child's welfare of a frightening, painful punishment at the hands of an adult.

On the other hand, if you want your parents to buy you this year's fashions and they say they can't afford it; that may be unpleasant, but it's not physical neglect. Your health and welfare are not at stake. But if your parents won't buy you a winter coat and you're wearing only a sweater in freezing weather, or if you're a boy and your parents insist on giving you a woman's coat, that's physical neglect. Your health and welfare are being threatened by this treatment.

Here's a list of some common forms of physical abuse and neglect.

Physical Abuse

- Any physical contact that leaves marks, bruises, or broken bones.
- Hitting with fists, weapons, or objects, such as a lamp, a poker, a heavy frying pan, or an extension cord. Beatings with a switch, a stick, or a strap are likely to be abusive, as well, particularly if they leave scars, welts, or large bruises.
- Burns, such as from boiling water, lye, or hot fat.
- Shaking someone violently, particularly a small child.
- Strangling or choking.
- Throwing someone down the stairs, into a wall, or into a piece of furniture; knocking someone to the ground.

- Forcing someone to stand or sit in an uncomfortable position or in a frightening place, such as a dark closet or a small, locked room.
- Tying someone up.
- Depriving someone of food or sleep as a punishment; demanding that someone undergo some kind of physical hardship as a punishment, such as walking a long distance in the cold or performing an unnecessarily dirty or dangerous task.

Some of the behavior we've just described may be presented to the child as a punishment. Some may seem to be the lashing out of an angry parent, or possibly of a parent who has been drinking or doing drugs. No matter what the provocation, no matter what the condition of the adult who performs these actions, *this behavior counts as abuse.*

Sometimes children find it hard to believe that their parents are hurting them so badly. It's easier to believe that there must be some good reason for the parent's behavior. If an adult presents this abuse as punishment, the child may try to justify the adult's behavior in his or her mind. "Yes," this child may think, "this punishment hurts a lot, but after all, I *was* careless. That was the third time I came home past curfew and Mom was worried. I guess I can see why she punishes me."

It's important to see that there is *no* good reason for an adult to injure a child or teenager that he or she is responsible for. There is no good reason for the health or welfare of a child or teen to be threatened. The child may have done nothing at all, and the parent may be inventing a reason to punish because of his or her need to be abusive. Or the child may have done something trivial, like spilling a glass of milk on the good tablecloth, which doesn't warrant severe punishment. The child may even have done something serious, like staying out all night, which may warrant severe punishment—but not abusive punishment.

Likewise, a child or teen may try to understand the parent whose abuse comes in the form of "lashing out." "Dad was tired," this teen may think. "He works all night at that lousy job. I can see why he'd be mad if I woke him up." The father's anger may be justified—but his abuse is not. It's possible to express anger without acting abusively—without threatening the health or welfare of your child.

Physical Neglect

Here are some examples of physical neglect. Once again, this behavior counts as neglect, no matter how good a reason a parent seems to have for acting this way.

- Not providing children with adequate food and shelter. (Of course if parents themselves don't have adequate food or shelter, as, say, homeless people do not, this is not child abuse but rather the effects of poverty. The family may still need help—but not help for abuse or neglect.)
- Not providing clothing that is generally appropriate to a child's age and sex, as well as to the weather and the environment.
- Not being physically present to supervise young children without finding a responsible adult or teenager to do so.
- Requiring an older child or teenager to spend long hours (more than one or two hours a day, regularly) in supervising younger brothers and sisters.
- Requiring children to do an inappropriate amount of the cooking, cleaning, and housekeeping because the parent is elsewhere or is physically incapable of doing anything. (We know that "inappropriate amount" is vague—and we certainly don't mean that it's neglect for a teenager to cook dinner while the parents are at work, or for children of all ages to have some chores! But if children must do work that is physically difficult or dangerous for their age, or if they have far more household responsibilities than a parent, that may be neglect.)

Physical neglect is often the result of poverty, or of a substance abuse problem—and sometimes both. If a single parent must go on a job interview, for example, and can't afford a baby-sitter, she may be tempted to leave young children alone in the house. The mother may even know that this is dangerous for the children— but she may also feel that she has no other choice.

When it comes to the physical neglect of teenagers, the situation becomes even more complicated. Teenagers are old enough to be given some adult-like responsibilities—but they aren't old enough to be treated like full-fledged adults. A teenager can reasonably be expected to take a part-time job, supervise younger brothers and sisters to some extent, and do some household chores. But teenagers should not be in the position of financially supporting a family or being the primary caretaker for younger brothers and sisters. Whether this is being done out of dire necessity or because the parent is acting irresponsibly doesn't change the reality: The teenager is being given more than he or she can handle. No matter what the parent's reasons for the neglect, the teenager needs and deserves help.

Emotional Abuse and Neglect

This type of abuse/neglect is probably the hardest of all to identify—though it may ultimately be as damaging as any other kind of abuse that doesn't result in death. Physical and sexual abuse are against the law and may be responded to by medical and social service authorities, or even by the police. Emotional abuse is much more subtle, and is not against the law. However, it is possible for the emotionally abused teen to get help, from others and from himself or herself. If the following discussion rings any bells with you, keep reading. Then take a special look at chapter 3, where we talk more about some ways for people in this category to get the help they need and deserve.

Emotional Abuse

For a starting point of emotional abuse, let's go back to the U.S. Congress definition and look at the parts that apply: "[any] mental injury . . . negligent treatment or maltreatment of a child under the age of 18 by a person who is responsible for the child's welfare under circumstances which indicate that the child's health or welfare is harmed or threatened thereby."

What does this mean? It means that Congress considers *mental* injury to be as significant as physical injury, especially when the injury comes from someone who has been trusted with the welfare of a child.

Another definition of emotional abuse refers to the "emotional survival of a child." This means that even if the child's body is safe, his or her *feelings* and *emotions* are being attacked. Sometimes this can hurt more than a physical attack, especially if the attacker is someone the child loves and whom the child depends on to take care of him or her.

In general, emotional abuse is behavior that undermines a child's self-confidence. Forcing a child to dress in clothing that's not appropriate to his or her age or sex is a humiliating experience. It may not leave a scar on a child's body, but it hurts nonetheless. Likewise, constantly telling a child that she or he is stupid, clumsy, in the way, an "accident," an embarrassment, difficult, not as good as someone else, or otherwise deficient is emotional abuse.

Children who are treated in these ways will have a very difficult time facing work and social situations with any kind of confidence in themselves. Since the people they love and depend on are treating them so badly, they will come to believe that they do not deserve to be treated well. Since the most important people in their lives are telling them that they are stupid or worthless, how are they supposed to believe anything else?

Another kind of emotional abuse mixes insults or humiliations with expressions of love. The parent may be insulting one minute, then full of praise the next. Perhaps the parent denies his or her insults, claiming, "I'm only teasing." Or perhaps the parent continues to be angry and insulting until the child is upset, when the parent suddenly rushes to comfort the child and apologize.

What the child learns from this is that people cannot be trusted. The person who acts loving one minute may humiliate you the next. Worse, the child learns that his or her own perceptions cannot be trusted. It's clear to the child that a parent is behaving in an angry or insulting way—but when the child responds accordingly, the parent tries to pretend that nothing happened, either by saying "I was just teasing" or by suddenly acting loving and apologetic.

Another category of emotional abuse involves the parent who acts as though she or he were the child, expecting the child to act like a parent. One elementary school child actually stole food for her mother from the cafeteria, because she knew that when she got home from school, her mother's first question would be "What did you bring me?" This child was being emotionally abused: She was being expected to always think of her mother first and herself second, as though her mother were a little baby who needed constant care and as though she herself were a grown-up who was ready to be a mother.

Because this child was not allowed to think of herself, she got the message that she herself was not a lovable person. She was being taught that she would only be loved according to how well she could take care of another person. Other children get the message that their parents don't care about *them*, only about their accomplishments. They too are being taught that they are not lovable in themselves, but only for what they can do for others—in this case, to make their parents feel proud.

Emotional abuse is common in families with one or more alcoholic or drug-addicted adults, whose addictions make them physically incapable of adequately caring for children. Children in these families often become "little parents." Unlike physical or sexual abuse, emotional abuse may well be a direct result of a parent's use of alcohol or drugs.

Here are some more examples of emotional abuse.

- Belittling someone's accomplishments, either by comparing them to another person's, or by explaining why the accomplishment doesn't mean much, will not last, or was probably an accident.
- Acting in one way and claiming to act in another, also known as *denial.* This includes parents who have drug or alcohol problems, or whose spouses do, while denying that there is a problem. It also includes parents who claim that they "never get angry"; parents who claim that they never think of themselves but only of their children; and parents who follow a burst of anger or insults with a round of apparently loving or apologetic behavior.
- Parents who are never satisfied, no matter how they express this dissatisfaction.

As we have seen, sometimes the children of physically abusive parents try to pretend that the abuse isn't really happening, even though they have scars and other physical evidence of their beatings. They act this way because it's less painful to pretend than to admit the truth: Their parents are hurting them.

If this pretending is possible even when there are actual physical events, imagine how much more difficult it is for children to face the truth about emotional abuse. One of the worst effects of emotional abuse is that it teaches children to doubt their own perceptions. They are supposed to believe that their parents love them—and the parents may even say that they love their children. At the same time, these loving parents are acting in ways that children know in their heart is not loving at all. Who are the children supposed to believe—themselves or their parents?

If this description fits you or someone you know, we encourage you or your friend to start believing yourself. It may be difficult and painful. It may even cause more trouble at home. But you have the right to trust yourself and your perceptions.

Emotional Neglect

Like emotional abuse, emotional neglect is hard to define and hard to identify—but it is very keenly felt by the children and teenagers who are its targets. Emotionally neglected children sense that they are not loved. No matter that their parents are physically present—somehow, they seem to be just "not quite there." No matter that their parents give them wonderful presents and frequently say "I love you" or "I'm proud of you"—somehow, the child or the teenager senses that this is not true.

If you saw the movie or read the book *Ordinary People*, you know one very good example of emotional neglect. The boy in that family knew that his mother didn't really care for him. She cared more about keeping up the appearance of a happy family than about loving him. Although she said she loved him, she didn't really want to hear his feelings or spend time with him. Instead, she wanted to pretend that everything was all right, and she wanted her son to pretend along with her. But because she never did or said anything "wrong" and because she claimed that she loved her son, it was very difficult for her son to identify the problem. He only *felt* that something was wrong.

As with other forms of abuse, children who are emotionally neglected may find it easier to blame themselves than to hold their parents responsible. They may prefer to think that there is something wrong with them, something that is either causing the parent to neglect them or that is preventing them from feeling the love the parents seems to offer. Or they may resent their parents, and even be able to express their anger at the emotional neglect—but underneath, they have also absorbed the message that something is wrong with them.

For teenagers who are emotionally neglected, or who were neglected as children, sometimes the greatest relief comes from telling the truth, to oneself, and, if possible, to someone else. Sometimes just being able to say "I know my mother doesn't love me" or "I'm so angry that my father doesn't care about me" can be an enormous release. This release may bring some grief and pain—but it may also free the teenager to look for new relationships with adults that are more satisfying.

Sexual Abuse

The other types of abuse we've been discussing have been focused on parent-child relations. Sexual abuse is somewhat different, in that the abuser may also be a teacher, baby-sitter, relative, sibling, family friend, or even a stranger. There are many definitions of sexual abuse, but perhaps the one offered by the National Center on Child Abuse and Neglect (NCCAN) is the most comprehensive:

> Contacts or interactions between a child and an adult when the child is being used for the sexual stimulation of the perpetrator or another person. Sexual abuse may also be committed by a person under the age of 18 when that person is either significantly older than the victim or when the perpetrator is in a position of power or control over the other child.

Sexual abuse, though very different from physical or emotional abuse, does have two things in common with these other types of abuse: The abuser often expects the abused person to keep the event a secret, and the abused person may decide that he or she is somehow to blame for the abuser's actions. The second is especially likely if the abuser is a parent or in some other way very close to the abused person. That's because, generally speaking, the closer you are to someone, the more difficult it is to accept that the person has hurt you. It may seem easier to blame yourself.

As with the other types of abuse, however, it should be stressed that *nothing* that a child or teenager does excuses sexual abuse on the part of an adult or an older teenager. Even if a child or a teenager were to literally ask a person in authority to engage in sexual behavior, it would still be the authority figure's responsibility to set appropriate limits.

Also, as with other types of abuse, it's important to identify that if some behavior makes you uncomfortable, it counts as sexual abuse. Sexual abuse is more than just the act of intercourse. It may include any of the actions on the following list, provided they take place between an adult and a person under 18, or between a teenager and a younger child.

- Being spied on or openly watched while you are dressing or undressing, bathing, using the bathroom, or doing some other activity normally performed in private. (Of course, such activity *is* appropriate with young children—and sometimes adults or baby-sitters just don't know when it's appropriate to back off. However, if their actions are not abusive, it should be easy to end the behavior by saying "I need some privacy now.")
- Being asked to watch someone else dress, undress, bathe, use the bathroom, or engage in some other private activity—or being put in a position where you can't help but see the other person engaged in these activities.
- Being tickled, caressed, hugged, or played with in a way that makes you uncomfortable.
- Engaging in any activity with a man in which you're aware that the man is getting an erection.
- Hearing someone "talk dirty" or having someone ask you to "talk dirty."
- Being asked explicit questions about your sexual activities or your relations with a boyfriend or girlfriend, or being told explicit details about another person's activities that you would rather not hear.
- Kissing that feels invasive or unwanted; "French," "tongue," or "soul" kissing.

- Having someone expose genitals or other sexual areas of the body to you, such as breasts or buttocks; being asked to expose sexual areas of your body.
- Being asked to touch the sexual areas of someone's body, or actually touching them; having someone touch these areas of your body. (Again, the appropriateness of this varies with a child's age—but if the action is not abusive, it should stop as soon as you request it to stop.)
- Oral-genital contact of any kind.

One of the problems teenagers often have in identifying sexual abuse is that behavior that was appropriate for them when they were children may no longer be appropriate once they've reached puberty. It's natural for a father to give his three-year-old daughter a bath and to help her wash herself. But when the daughter is 13, such behavior is a real invasion of her privacy. A 10-year-old boy may enjoy playing a chasing and tickling game with his aunt. The same tickling with a 14-year-old nephew may arouse uncomfortable feelings.

If a relative, parent, or family friend is engaging in such invasive behavior, you may have the feeling that something is wrong without quite knowing what it is. After all, you, too, are used to a close physical relationship with this person. And if the other person, a grown-up, insists that you are being foolish and that nothing is wrong, it may be difficult for you to stick to your guns and insist on the truth of your own feelings. It's important for you to know that no one else has the right to judge with what you should and should not be comfortable: *You* are the only judge of that, and you have the right to protect yourself.

Another type of sexual abuse is even more subtle and still more difficult to identify. It occurs when the entire atmosphere of a home is somehow sexualized, when everything seems to have sexual meaning, even if there is no overtly inappropriate touching or exposure. If you are living in or visiting such a home, you may sense that something is wrong without being able to say specifically what it is. Perhaps you feel that an affectionate kiss good-bye on the cheek has taken on another meaning or is found to be sexually exciting by the other person, when you were expressing not sex but only affection. Or perhaps you feel that your affectionate hugs and kisses are pushed away with as much disapproval as if you were a sexual and seductive adult, rather than an affectionate child.

This type of atmosphere can be very confusing. You start out knowing what you feel—but somehow you realize that the adults in your life are acting as though you felt something else. Whom do you believe—them or yourself? If this has been your experience, learning to trust yourself and to believe in your own feelings will be very important for you.

Abuse and Teenagers

Abuse is an issue that affects children of all ages, but it brings up special problems for teenagers. Approximately half the adolescents being abused today were also abused as children. Although these teens have grown up with abuse, they are no longer the same helpless children that they once were. They are stronger and smarter, and, even more importantly, they have more resources outside the home. Unlike infants and toddlers, abused teens are probably aware that not everyone's family acts abusively, or, in the case of sexual abuse, that not every adult or teenager is guilty of abuse.

However, these additional outside resources may put the teenager into even greater conflict. Even though the teen is closer to being an adult than before, he or she is not yet fully grown up. In most cases, teenagers can't earn enough money to support themselves away from the family home. They don't have the same legal status as adults, and they may have less credibility than an adult. Teenagers are still subject to adult authority in most spheres of their life. Thus a teenager may still not have the power to end physical, emotional, or sexual abuse by himself or herself, even though he or she may be more ready to take action than before.

This means that teenagers still need to find an adult to help them end the abuse. Being older and more articulate, a teenager has more resources to find adult help than before. But a teenager may not see it this way. Teens may think that they *should* be able to end the abuse themselves, now that they're aware of it, and so they may feel guilty and self-blaming if the abuse continues. It might be difficult for teens to accept that they may still need adult help to end the abuse.

In some cases, teens are successful in ending physical or sexual abuse by themselves. A physically powerful teen may be able to stop a parent from battering him or her. A teen who threatens the sexually abusing person that he or she will "tell," or who simply has the resources to say no, may be able to end the abusive part of the relationship. And some sexual abusers stop themselves when the abused person reaches adolescence. They may then go on to abuse another, younger person—but the abusive relationship with the teenager may end.

However, even if the actual abusive actions stop, the effects of the abuse do not. The lasting effects of sexual abuse are very deep and powerful. It's not enough for the abuse to stop; the person who has been abused must work through all of his or her feelings about what happened, whether the abuse was physical, emotional, or sexual. If the feelings are ignored or suppressed, they will almost certainly continue to affect the person's life.

Chapter 3 includes a full discussion about how to work through these feelings. For now, let's just point out that if you or someone you know was ever abused, you may still need help in working through the experience.

What about the other half of the picture, the teens who are abused in some way for the first time after the age of 13? Abuse that begins when the child is older stems from the changes of adolescence. For example, teenagers becoming physically stronger may lead some parents to escalate from "ordinary" physical punishments into violence: A 10-year-old may be subdued by a spanking, whereas a teenager may be controlled only by more severe beating.

Another factor of adolescence that can provoke abuse is that the teenage years are a time of asking questions, challenging authority, and seeking greater independence. Parents who seek to maintain control over their children may find this threatening. They may resort to physical or emotional abuse to "manage" the child who, for the first time, has the resources to answer back, to argue, and to bring in information about how other families operate.

Some sexual abusers may ignore a child until he or she has reached puberty. The abuser may then see a teenager's growing sexuality as an invitation that gives permission to act abusively.

Of course, this perception is distorted. All humans develop sexually around the early teen years: this isn't an "invitation," but a simple fact of life. But a teenager who is struggling to understand his or her sexual feelings may be confused by the person who says "I know what you want" or "You acted like you wanted this—why are you changing your mind now?" If the adult who says this has enough authority, the teenager may come to doubt his or her own feelings and may believes that the adult really does know more about what's going on. This may be even more likely if the teen has been taught to obey his or her elders or to believe that grown-ups know best.

Finally, as we've seen, many abused children have come to believe that they are somehow responsible for their parents. Many abusive parents do act like children and expect their children to act like parents. As children become teenagers and are in fact capable of acting more like adults, it might seem to the teenager that he or she really *could* fill an adult's place. This may make the teen feel guilty or confused about refusing a parents' demands. A teenage boy being told that he's "the man of the house" or a teenage girl being told that she's "our little wife and mother" may have a harder time saying "But I'm not ready to be a husband or wife, I'm not ready to be a father or mother—I'm still growing up!" The fact that the teenager is so much closer to being a grown-up may hide the fact that, after all, he or she still isn't ready for adult responsibilities and still deserves adult support and guidance.

Even if some teenagers are fully ready to take care of themselves, there's no reason why they must then be expected to take care of their parents. Certainly they should not be expected to "take care" of a parent sexually, or to accept physical or emotional abuse from parents because the parents "can't help" themselves.

Power and Abuse: Who Can Be an Abuser?

Child abuse is a painful topic. Sometimes people try to minimize that pain by making the problem seem smaller than it is. One way of doing this is by assuming that only "certain types" of people can be abusers. Those "certain types" are almost always *other* people—strangers, monsters, people in a different social group—"certainly not anyone *we* know!"

The truth is, people who engage in child abuse can be found in all social groups. They are of all races, religions, and ages; they are in big cities and small towns and farms and suburbs; they are of all educational and income levels. People who abuse children can be either men or women, and either sex may abuse boys or girls. Child abuse is a very widespread problem and no group is inherently immune to it.

It's also true that we can't draw a sharp line between child abusers and "the rest of us." Everyone has the capacity to act abusively. In fact, one estimate says that some 90 percent of all parents engage in physical or emotional abuse at least once in their lives.

If so many people may act abusively, does this mean that the targets of abuse should accept their treatment as "normal" and not complain? Certainly not. Just because anyone *can* be an abuser doesn't mean that everyone *is* an abuser. A child's receiving abusive treatment only once or twice in his or her life may be serious, depending on the circumstances. But if a child is subjected to a regular pattern of abusive behavior, it is a very serious problem.

Parents don't have the obligation to be perfect, but they do have the obligation not to harm the health or welfare of their children. Parents who abuse their children need help to stop the abusive pattern, and children who are being abused need the abuse to stop immediately.

Another way that people sometimes try to minimize the pain of child abuse is to say that the abusive action is really something else. They say that physical abuse is really "discipline," that emotional abuse is merely "criticism," and that sexual abuse is actually an expression of sexual feelings and affection.

To describe abuse in this way makes it sound as though the abuser is simply trying to meet a child's needs for love or guidance. But abuse does not come from trying to meet a child's needs. Abuse may come from many motives—an adult's own pent-up rage and frustration, parents' needs to push negative feelings about themselves off onto their children, an adult's or teen's wish for love and affection. Whatever the motives, however, the behavior is abusive, because it comes from the older person's needs, not the child's—and because it takes advantage of the older person's power over the child.

The parent who beats, criticizes unmercifully, or engages in sexual behavior with a child may be convinced that he or she is acting in the child's bests interests. And the child may genuinely need discipline or criticism or affection of some kind. But the real motive for abuse comes from the adult's needs, not the child's. The abusive adult—or, in some cases, the abusive teenager—has chosen to exercise power over a younger person who depends on him or her. That isn't love or discipline or help—it's an exercise of power.

Why Do Abusers Act the Way They Do?

If child abusers aren't monsters, then why do they act the way they do? If we believe that some of them, at least, love the children they abuse, how do we understand their actions?

There's no one answer to these questions, but there are some explanations that may help us understand. First, some abusers may simply not know any other way to act. This is particularly true of parents who physically abuse or neglect infants. Some parents, particularly young or teenage parents, don't have a realistic idea of how easily an infant can be hurt or of how much stronger they are than their babies. They don't realize how unsafe it is to leave infants or toddlers alone in the house or how damaging it is to tie them to a bed to "protect" them while the parent goes out. These parents need education and help to enable them to act differently.

With other abusive parents, the problem goes deeper. Many child abusers were also survivors of child abuse themselves. If they were physically, emotionally, or sexually abused as children, or possibly if they grew up with someone who was abused, they may grow up to repeat the abuse as adults.

Some people in this category are simply unaware of any other way of acting. They may believe that it's normal to beat a child or to vent one's anger with harsh insults. They may believe that it's normal to engage in sexually abusive behavior, since that's what they grew up with.

For many parents who were abused as children, their reason for abusing their own children is that they need to prove that their parents were right. They do this by treating their children exactly as their parents treated them. You'll recall that many children find it easier to pretend that they are somehow responsible for the abuse, or that their parents are acting out of love, rather than to hold their parents responsible for acting badly. When those children grow up, they still don't want to admit that their parents acted badly. So they act just like their parents, because, they reason to themselves, their parents were acting out of love.

Sometimes these parents decide that their children "deserve" to be abused, just like they "deserved" it when *they* were kids. Sometimes these parents identify with their own parents: "He got to beat me, so now I get to beat you—it's my turn now." Sometimes children remind parents of someone who abused them or someone whom they're angry at, such as a husband who left home. Parents may not be aware that they're taking out their feelings against this person on a child who in reality has done nothing wrong.

In addition, people who were abused as children would generally have felt very helpless as they grew up. After all, the adults that they depended on were not very dependable—instead, they were abusive. When these children become adults, they still have the feeling of being helpless and abused by a powerful, angry person. In this frame of mind, they often perceive children or growing teenagers as a "powerful" person.

In reality, of course, a parent is always much more powerful than a child. But in his or her own mind, the parent feels like a child, and the crying baby or the arguing teenager seems to have all the power of an angry father or mother. So the parent feels justified in doing anything to make this seemingly powerful person "behave."

No matter how much they may love their parents, abused children probably also feel anger and resentment, along with the love. So when these children grow up, they may still feel angry and resentful that they weren't treated properly. They may still be waiting for someone to come along and treat them like a loving parent, instead of an abusive one. They may even expect that they will get this kind of love from their children. But children cannot act like loving parents since they are not old enough. So all of the parent's leftover anger against his or her own parents gets let out on the child, even though the child has done nothing to deserve it.

Parents who expected only love and caring from their children may be very frustrated when they discover that little babies have needs of their own. One young mother who abandoned her child later said, "I thought that finally someone would love me, but this baby is always crying—he doesn't love me, either." In reality the baby was crying because he was hungry or tired or wanted something. But the mother could only see her own need to be loved, and therefore misinterpreted her baby's actions, which led her to act abusively.

This pattern is also experienced by emotionally abusive parents. Even though these parents may not batter their children, they may make inappropriate demands on them. Because the parents felt unloved as children, they want their children to make up for it. But a child cannot make up for a parent's disappointments. So both parent and child continue to be frustrated and hurt. And the parent continues to take that frustration out on the child by making unfair demands or expressing unfair criticisms.

Sometimes emotionally abusive parents who themselves were deprived as children may unconsciously resent the idea that anyone will get something they themselves were denied. They may also simply not know how to give emotional support, since they themselves never got any. They may feel so deprived of love themselves that they cannot conceive of how to love their own children. Or they may love their children, but not be able to provide a sense of security, respect, or any other quality that was missing from their own childhood.

Sexual abusers were often sexually abused themselves as children. Again, they may be trying to make up for the experience, proving to themselves that the adults who abused them "weren't so bad" by imitating those adults.

Some sexually abusive adults and teenagers may feel that no one loves them or cares about them. They may feel that everyone their own age dislikes them or doesn't love them enough. It may scare them that they cannot control these other people, that they cannot make sure that the people they love will love them back the way they'd like. Such people may feel that in a sexual relationship with a child they have finally found someone to love them—someone whom they can also control. Because a child is so dependent on adults (and on teenage authorities like baby-sitters), and because a child or a teenager knows less and has less power than an adult, that younger person will be far more easy to control than someone of the abuser's own age. So the abuser feels safer with the younger person.

Such abusers may lie to themselves, telling themselves that the younger person wants the relationship as much as they do. In fact, the abusers are using their power to get the love that they fear they can't get in any other way.

What About the Other Parent?

Frequently in families only one parent is abusive, and the other parent does not act abusively. What about these other parents? If they aren't abusers themselves, how can they allow abuse to go on?

Again, this is a complicated question and there's no one simple answer. In the case of physical abuse, the nonabusive parent may also be scared of or abused by the battering parent. Especially in the case of battering men, wives and children may be equally at risk.

In this case, the mother may have many different reasons for going along with the abuse. She may believe that she deserves to be beaten, perhaps because she too was an abused child. She may believe that someday the man will stop, and that meanwhile, he really loves her—which may also be feelings that she had about a battering parent when she was a child. Since as a child she was powerless to stop the abuse of her parents, she may not realize that as an adult she has more power than before. She may not realize that even if she can't stop the abuse, she could leave the abuser—an option she didn't have as a child.

Or the mother may want to leave, but not know how she'll financially support the family without a man. She may also believe, perhaps correctly, that the battering man will hurt her and the children even more severely if she leaves.

A man whose wife is physically abusive is less likely to be physically frightened of her or economically dependent on her. But he may still feel powerless to affect her actions. Again, if he grew up with an abusive mother, he may still carry around those childlike feelings of being helpless and dependent. He may not realize that he could affect the actions of his wife in a way that he could not affect the actions of his mother. He may not realize that as an adult, he can leave the house and take his children with him—since he certainly couldn't act that way as a child.

A nonabusive parent of either sex may also believe that the abusing parent is acting "correctly." Again, this may well go back to their own experiences as children. If as children they believed that their parents knew best and that they themselves knew nothing, it may be easy to continue those feelings as adults and decide that another parent "knows best."

Sometimes a nonabusive parent is aware of the children's pain, but still feels more loyal to the other adult. If that parent is not willing to lose the relationship with the abuser, he or she will not be willing to challenge the abuser or insist that the abuse stop.

Such a parent may try to "make things better" by comforting children after the abuse, or by trying to help them learn how to avoid "making Daddy or [Mommy] angry." Unfortunately, this behavior usually doesn't prevent abuse—because the child's behavior was never really the cause of the abuse. However, the child may get the message from the nonabusive parent that somehow he or she *is* causing the trouble. The child may believe that if only he or she could be "good" enough, the abuse would stop. Even though the nonabusive parent isn't hitting the child, he or she is reinforcing a negative message.

The nonabusive parent may also try to make the child feel sorry for the abusing parent. The child may be told that "Daddy can't help it" or "You know that Mommy loves you even if she hits you."

Unfortunately, this also carries a negative message. Children are being told that they are loved by a person who has just finished battering or abusing them. They may get the message that anyone who loves them will also beat or abuse them. Or they may get the message that they should feel sorry for the abusing parents, rather than angry with them. Instead of learning to defend themselves against bad treatment, these children are being taught to take the side of the abuser and to look at things from his or her point of view. This may make it difficult for them later, when they meet abusive people who are *not* their parents.

These patterns also apply to emotional and sexual abuse to some extent. If a mother lets loose a stream of unfair criticism, a child's natural reaction would probably be to get mad and tell her to stop. But if the father is saying "Don't get mad—you know she doesn't mean it," then the child becomes confused. It sounded like she meant it. It hurt as much as if she meant it. What is the child supposed to do with the hurt and angry feelings?

Thus, even if the other parent is not directly abusing the child, he or she may be contributing to the feeling that the child is somehow responsible for the abuse. Children need their parents for protection, and for an accurate view of reality. One of the bad effects of abuse is that it teaches children that their parents will not protect them, and that their parents will not tell them the truth about reality. Instead, both their parents, whether abusive or not, ask the child to believe that the child's own feelings don't count and that the child's perceptions of reality aren't accurate.

The pattern may be the same with sexual abuse if the other parent is aware of the abuse. However, because of the secrecy that frequently surrounds sexual abuse, a parent may not be aware that a child has been abused. The child may also be unsure whether the parent is aware or not.

If a child or teenager has been sexually abused by someone who is not living in the home, it's quite possible that the parents are not aware. Even in that case, the child's decision whether to tell them will be influenced by the messages that these parents have given. If the parents have encouraged their child to trust his or her own perceptions and to stand up for his or her rights, the child may feel more secure in telling about what happened and asking the parents for support. (Children who have been threatened with physical harm to themselves or to others may also be unwilling to tell their parents, regardless of how good the relationship is.) If these parents have encouraged the child to believe that anything bad that happens is somehow the child's fault, the child will be a lot less likely to turn to the parents for help. Rightly or wrongly, such a child may fear that he or she will be blamed for having been abused.

If you or someone you know is in such a situation, we encourage you to find an adult that you do trust. This person will almost certainly tell your parents, but at least you will have the support of another adult and you will have taken an important step toward stopping the abuse.

What about when the child or teenager is abused by someone within the home? This is an even more complicated situation. If the father or stepfather is abusing the child, the mother may be unwilling to end the relationship, for all the reasons we discussed above. Therefore, although the mother may suspect that something is going on, she may wish to hide the truth, even from herself.

Of course, sometimes the nonabusive parent is genuinely unaware of any abuse. Sometimes, too, a parent will be aware of the abuse but will choose not to do anything about it, out of fear, insecurity, a sense of helplessness and despair, or some other motive. Sometimes, though, nonabusive parents try to "not know," to deny or ignore the truth.

This wish to hide the truth is a common and complicated dynamic in many families. The mother may do her best not to notice evidence of abuse—for example, to ignore the fact that the man of the house is actually in a child's bedroom, or not to notice that a child's blouse is buttoned wrong when the mother comes home unexpectedly. After all, these are things that a person actually might not notice.

Perhaps the mother sees evidence of abuse that she cannot ignore. So she tells herself that "it doesn't mean anything" or that she is "imagining things." If her need to preserve the relationship with the man is great enough, she may do a great deal to avoid knowing the truth, either by not noticing things or by explaining them away.

Sometimes, when such a mother is finally confronted with the truth, she is still unwilling to end the relationship with the abusive man. If so, she may decide to blame the child, rather than to hold the adult man responsible for his actions. The mother is acting out of her own fears and needs, rather than correctly perceiving reality and acting in the best interests of her child.

Likewise, the husband of an abusive mother or stepmother may be unwilling to end the relationship. He too may ignore or lie to himself about the sexual abuse taking place in his home. He too may blame the abused person rather than the abuser if he is finally confronted with the truth.

As with the other examples, the nonabusive parent may mistakenly try to make things better by advising the child to "stay out of his way" or "don't wear that shirt." The parent may be trying to help—but the child gets the message that he or she is to blame for the abuse, rather than the real culprit.

It's difficult to accept that, whatever their intentions, your parents aren't really protecting your health and welfare the way they're supposed to. However, if this *is* true, it's less painful in the long run to face the truth. Finding other adults whom you do trust is one step in being able to stop the abuse and then to work through your feelings about it.

Child Abuse and Substance Abuse

Frequently, in those families where child abuse is taking place, substance abuse is also a problem. One or both parents drinks or abuses drugs and then abuses one or more children while drunk or high.

Many of the patterns we've been discussing are further emphasized by the presence of substance abuse. For example, parents with drug or alcohol problems may "need" children to care for them. Because they are drunk, high, hungover, or coming down, they may be physically incapable of caring for themselves or for the children. In some two-parent families, one adult has the substance abuse problem while the other is completely focused on caring for "the problem adult," rather than having time or energy to care for the children. Thus the children suffer from physical or emotional neglect.

If the substance abuser only batters or sexually abuses the child when he or she is high, the child may be encouraged to believe that the parent is not responsible for his or her actions—it's just "the liquor talking" or what the drug "made me do." If there are two adults, one may encourage the child to forgive or feel sorry for the abusing parent citing the drugs or alcohol as an excuse for the abusive behavior. The child is in the same double bind we discussed above: He or she is angry with the abusing parent, but is not allowed to express that feeling or to identify the real problem of abuse. Instead, the child is expected to feel sorry for the abusing parent, at the cost of denying his or her own feelings.

Just as some parents ask their children to pretend that they're not being abused, so some parents ask their children to pretend that no one in the family has a drug or alcohol problem. The child is not allowed to say that "Daddy is drunk" or "Mommy is high"; instead, the child is supposed to say that "Daddy is tired" or "Mommy is sick." Once again, the child is being asked to deny his or her own perceptions, and to focus on the parent's need instead of his or her own.

Just as abusive parents are acting out of their own fears and needs, so are parents with substance abuse problems. Just as abusive parents may have been abused as children, substance abusers may have grown up with alcoholic or addicted parents. It may help a child to understand that parents are acting out of their own problems, rather than because of something the child has done.

However, it's also important to hold adults responsible for their actions. Adults don't act abusively because they get drunk or high. Many adults have drug or alcohol problems and do not then abuse the children they live with. As we discussed before, drugs and liquor don't create the impulse to physically, sexually, or emotionally abuse. They merely make it easier for the adult to act on that impulse. Drugs and liquor *may* create the impulse to neglect children—but even so, the adults are still responsible for their actions. They are responsible for addressing their addictions so that they can adequately care for their children.

If you or someone you know is living with abusive parents who also have a drug or alcohol problem, we encourage you to seek help from groups like Al-Anon, and Al-A-Teen, or from Nar-Anon and Nar-A-Teen, all of which can be located in the white pages of the phone directory by contacting Al-Anon. Such groups will help you to understand that you are not responsible for your parents' behavior—but you are responsible for your own. You may not be able to get your parents to look for the help they need, but *you* can look for the help that *you* need.

Working with groups like Al-Anon has another benefit: it might put you in contact with adults and teenagers who may be able to support you in ending the abuse you are experiencing. The more relationships you can establish with supportive adults, the better. This will not come between you and your parents—it will make it easier for you to have the strength to deal responsibly with your parents.

Abuse, Privacy, and Community

We've been discussing some of the specific reasons why adults and teenagers turn to abuse. But there's one more general reason: a lack of community.

Many people in this country see the individual family as the basic unit of society. They believe that parents should be able to do everything necessary to take care of their children by themselves. These people see it as a sign of shame or failure if parents are having difficulties or if they need support from others.

However, many studies of child abuse suggest that isolation is a major factor. When families have difficulties, perhaps from unemployment or some other social problem, they may respond to their problem in a number of ways. The families that respond by isolating themselves, by withdrawing from friends and neighbors, are the most likely to be abusive.

Other studies have shown that abusive families tend to be more isolated than other families. They tend to have fewer friends, less contact with neighbors, and less access to resources such as the welfare system or social service system; churches, synagogues, and other religious groups; and other community organizations. Isolation seems to be both a cause and an effect of abusive patterns.

Likewise, the image of the family as a unit whose privacy must be respected at all costs often keeps people from intervening in families where abuse is taking place. The image that children are the property of their parents, rather than a responsibility of the entire society, keeps many children isolated in dangerous and abusive situations.

To us, this suggests that community is a necessary part of family life. Parents should not have to feel that they are completely alone or that they are failures if they turn to "outsiders" for help and support.

Likewise, if teenagers are growing up in abusive families, one of the best things they can do for themselves is to go outside the family to find other adults, people who can provide the support that the family is unable to provide. Unfortunately, because abused families are more likely to be isolated and to value the idea of "keeping it in the family," abused teens may feel guilty looking for outside support. And they may have difficulty meeting other adults, because of their own family's isolation.

If you or someone you know is in this situation, it helps to recall that going outside the family is not disloyal. It's simply the natural expression of people's wish for community—a healthy wish that makes families stronger, not weaker. If your family has isolated itself, you may have to create your own community. It may be difficult—but it will be worth it.

The Effects of Abuse

Now that we've looked more closely at the dynamics of abuse, let's go back to our composite stories of abused teenagers. How are they coping with the abuse? What effects are the various types of abuse having on their lives?

- Geneva tries hard to be the good girl her parents want her to be. She believes that if she were better, her father wouldn't beat her. But somehow, no matter how hard she tries, she always makes a mistake. She's starting to feel like she can't do anything right *anywhere.* When her friend Marlys asked her to work on the school paper, Geneva found that she was so nervous about trying something new that she couldn't even walk into the newspaper office. Another time, Geneva and a bunch of her friends went shopping together to buy food for a Halloween party. Geneva was supposed to buy a certain brand of apple cider. When she didn't show up at the cash register, her friends went looking for her. They found her standing by the shelf, waiting—the store was out of the brand they had agreed on, and Geneva was afraid to choose another brand by herself.

- Lou has never gotten good grades, and by this point his teachers don't even expect him to. But his guidance counselor thinks something is wrong somewhere, because when the entire school was given standard intelligence tests, Lou scored in the top ten percent. When the guidance counselor asked Lou what was wrong, Lou just shrugged and said he wasn't interested in school. What he does like to do is go drinking and driving with his friends, the faster the better. Lou is the best at thinking up new challenges, like driving around a sharp curve with no lights on or racing along the shoulder of the road. Lou thinks up other challenges too—like who can hold a lighted cigarette against his arm the longest. Lou almost always wins these contests, and he brags about how tough he is and how well he can "take it."

- Maria feels angry at her mother all the time. About the only time she's not mad is when she's eating. Maria loves to eat. Sometimes the only thing that keeps her going through the day is thinking about the candy bar she has stashed in her locker, or about the donut she'll buy on her way home from school. If Maria doesn't have the money to buy food, she'll try to steal it, because the one thing she's *not* going to give up is her treats. Because she eats so much, Maria has gained a lot of weight. Her younger brothers and sisters tease her about being so fat, and then Maria yells at them. Then she feels guilty. Plus she feels like even more of a failure—obviously, she can't do anything right.

Geneva, Lou, and Maria are all experiencing common effects from physical abuse and neglect. Geneva is experiencing a condition known as "learned helplessness." Since she has learned that she is helpless to prevent her father's beatings, she has decided that she is helpless to affect anything else. She is nervous about entering new situations because the most important situation in her life—her family—is not a safe place for her. Consequently, she doesn't expect to feel safe in any situation. She is nervous about making decisions on her own because her father's punishments for making the "wrong" decisions are so severe. Geneva copes with her lack of control over her father by giving up control over everything in her life, even situations or decisions that she rationally might expect to turn out differently.

Lou copes with his mother's physical abuse of him by physically abusing himself. He thinks if he can "train" himself to bear pain by burning himself with cigarettes, he can bear the pain of his mother's beatings—and the pain of her bad treatment. Because his mother treats Lou's physical safety so carelessly, Lou treats his own safety that way, too.

Like Geneva, Lou is basically unable to control his parent's actions. While Geneva dealt with this by giving up her control completely, Lou tries to take control back. But he does so by imitating his mother. It's as though he feels that if *he* is the one endangering his life, rather than her, he has some control over his safety.

Lou's difficulties in school are also a common pattern with abused children of all types. Some of the difficulties arise because it's not easy to study in a chaotic home where a violent argument or action may erupt at any moment. Some of the problem is caused by apathy—next to a parent who is endangering your welfare, school might not seem very important. Some of it is caused by anger—if your home life isn't working out, why should you try to make anything work out?

And some school difficulties may be a cry for help. Perhaps on some level, Lou hopes that his guidance counselor will notice that there's a problem and keep asking questions— even though Lou also resents the guidance counselor and refuses to answer his questions.

These contradictory feelings come from Lou's contradictory situation: On the one hand, he wants his mother to stop abusing him; on the other hand, he thinks he should protect her. Meanwhile, since she treats his safety carelessly, so does he.

Like Lou and Geneva, Maria is also unable to count on a very important person in her life. She, too, is looking for something to count on that she *can* control. In her case, it is food. Since Maria's mother won't feed her, Maria will feed herself. But since Maria wants much more than food from her mother, she'll never really be satisfied by eating. That's why she has to keep on eating, long after she's stopped being hungry—because the angry and sad feelings that the food was supposed to "fix" haven't really gone away.

Maria's problem is called an *eating disorder*. Emotionally and sexually abused children may also develop eating disorders. Maria's problem is known as *compulsive eating*—when a person feels like she has to keep eating and can't stop, whether she's hungry or not. Another type of eating disorder is known as *anorexia*—when a person diets so heavily that she literally starves herself, to the point where she has to go to the hospital. A related problem is called *bulimia*—when a person first eats compulsively, then makes herself throw up in order not to gain weight. Each of these problems is different, but they all have two things in common: They're all a way to cope with painful feelings, and they're all a way to try to control at least one area of your life. Unfortunately, they don't solve any real problems—and in the meantime, people with these disorders are in effect abusing themselves.

- Jerry gets good grades in school, but he can't seem to do much else. After he graduates, however, his parents finally do let him take a part-time job, as a stock clerk at a grocery store. But he gets fired on the second day. When the dairy case started leaking water, Jerry went to his supervisor to get help to wipe it up. When a customer knocked over a display of cans, Jerry went to his supervisor to ask how he was supposed to stack them up again. Then, when the supervisor laughed and asked Jerry why he couldn't figure it out on his own, Jerry became furious. He started yelling and screaming at the supervisor and almost threw a can at him. When the supervisor fired Jerry, Jerry calmed down at once and quietly went home.

- Elena finds herself thinking about death all the time. She reads books about people who are dying or about ghosts who come back from beyond the grave. She thinks about different ways of killing herself, although she'd never admit that she thinks this way. Lately, though, she's done more than just think about it. She's begun to check out different possibilities—like seeing if her mom has enough sleeping pills to cause a death. Elena feels like she can't control these thoughts of death—they just come and take over. She wonders if one day she actually will commit suicide.

- Seth gets along all right with the other guys in his class, although he doesn't really have any close friends. The other guys notice that whenever they're having a really hard time, Seth somehow makes some crack that makes them feel worse. Then he apologizes—but it's too late. The damage is done. When the other guys start going out on dates, Seth decides that he'd also like to have a girlfriend, but somehow, there's no one he really wants to go out with. Some of his other friends try to include him in double dates, but Seth always finds something to criticize in every girl. At the same time, Seth feels lonely and left out. He'd like to have a girlfriend, and he doesn't understand why no one wants to go out with him.

Jerry's parents have convinced him that he can't make any decisions on his own. They've also given him the message that if he does succeed away from home, they will feel left out and will be angry with him. So when Jerry does have a chance to gain more independence, he's too nervous to take it.

At the same time, Jerry feels an enormous amount of anger at his parents—anger that he's never been allowed to express. So the first chance he gets to be angry at someone else—in this case, his supervisor—he blows up. His supervisor did something that was a little bit like what his parents did—seeming to laugh at Jerry for not knowing what to do—and Jerry has so much stored-up anger about that, he can't deal with it rationally. Of course, once Jerry was fired, he was "fine"—*that* felt comfortable and familiar, and he was safe from the "threat" of independence. The emotional abuse that Jerry has taken has left him with very great difficulties in dealing with the world outside of his family.

Elena has another kind of problem. On some level, she has absorbed the message that since her parents don't love her, she must not deserve to be alive. Since she can't identify her problem consciously, she can't think about it rationally.

If Elena could trust her own feeling that her parents don't really love her, and if she could admit that truth to herself, she might feel a great deal of pain; but she might also be able to see another alternative. She might be able to say to herself, "Okay, so my parents don't love me. I'm still a lovable person. I'm going to keep on living until I find some other people who do love me the way I deserve. And, in the meantime, I'll learn to love myself."

Since Elena isn't yet willing or able to face the truth, she's got to look for another way to stop the pain. So suicide seems like her only escape. All kinds of abused children often have suicidal thoughts, and sometimes they act on them.

Unlike the other teenagers we've looked at, Seth doesn't seem to have any obvious problems. On the surface, he seems like an ordinary guy, one who gets along okay at school and with his friends.

Underneath, though, Seth is feeling the effects of his parents' emotional abuse, and his actions show these effects as well.

Seth has difficulty getting close to anyone because he expects the same criticisms and rejections he got from his parents. To protect himself, he criticizes everyone else—and so, of course, people don't want to get close to him. This confirms his fear that his parents are right, that there really is something wrong with him and that good times never last very long.

Children who are emotionally abused often have difficulty with close relationships. Physically and sexually abused children may have problems in this area, as well. When the most important people in a child's life—the parents—are not trustworthy, it becomes very difficult for the child to learn to trust anyone else. When the most important people in a child's life cause huge amounts of pain, it becomes difficult to be very optimistic about other relationships. And when the people who reflect your identity to you reflect only a negative picture, it is difficult to develop self-esteem. If you have no sense of your own value, how can you accurately perceive what your value is to others?

- When Suzy does start dating, she finds herself facing a number of contradictory feelings. Sometime she feels guilty without really knowing why. Other times she feels like she has a terrible secret, and that the boys she dates won't like her if they find out about it. Still other times, Suzy feels like the only reason boys like her is because they think she'll "put out" sexually, and she thinks she'd better go further than she wants to, just to be sure of getting asked out again. But when she does act sexual, she worries that the guys she's dating won't respect her. The one thing that Suzy *doesn't* feel is relaxed and happy about kissing and making out. She does get turned on—but her sexual feelings almost always make her feel guilty or nervous.

- Carlene isn't sure how much longer she can take her "double life." Sometimes she thinks the only solution is running away. She has fantasies about just getting on a bus and going off to another city. She thinks that if she just disappeared, she'd be free of the sexual abuse and she wouldn't get her family into trouble. Carlene's fantasies never have very many details. Usually, they only go as far as her getting on a bus and riding away.

- Marc never has any trouble getting a date. But now a lot of girls in school are mad at him. When Marc first goes out with a girl, he always likes her a lot. He's very sweet and attentive. He never actually makes specific promises, but he talks so much about the wonderful things they'll do together that the girl thinks he's very serious. Then, after he has sex with a girl a few times, he loses interest. Usually, neither he nor the girl quite realizes that he's lost interest— until she catches him with somebody else. Then she gets really mad and hurt. Marc's reputation isn't really making it hard for him to get dates—but he does feel bad about why so many people are mad at him. He also wonders why his relationships never last very long.

Suzy, Carlene, and Marc are all coping with sexual abuse in a common way. They are all trying to *deny* their experience, to somehow pretend that it didn't happen. This pattern of denial ends up creating new problems without really solving the core problem.

Suzy feels uncomfortable about her earlier experience with the baby-sitter. Perhaps because her parents have encouraged her to "mind her elders" and not to express angry feelings or criticisms, Suzy was afraid to tell her parents exactly what happened when she was eight. She was afraid they might blame her, maybe even punish her for doing something wrong.

Because she feels so uncomfortable about that early abusive experience, Suzy has tried to forget it. But she hasn't really forgotten it. She's only pushed it down out of sight. By doing this, she's giving herself a message: You did something wrong and you're a bad person. In fact, she's giving herself exactly the message that she was afraid that her parents would give to her.

By pushing her memories and her feelings out of sight, Suzy hasn't really gotten rid of them. Instead, she has all of those feelings about her *current* sexual experiences. She feels guilty for liking to kiss boys and make out with them, even though such activity is appropriate for a teenager. But because Suzy was not given a choice about being sexual with her baby-sitter when she was eight, it's hard for her to believe that she has the freedom to choose now.

Likewise, Suzy found it very confusing to enjoy her baby-sitter's sexual behavior with her, even though she also knew she wasn't comfortable with it. So she finds it confusing and upsetting to have sexual feelings now, even though now she *is* old enough to be more comfortable with some sexual behavior. Because Suzy hasn't really worked out her feelings about the past, she's getting those past feelings all mixed up with the present.

Carlene hasn't worked out her feelings about the past *or* the present. She's in such a painful, difficult situation that she can cope with it only by pretending to herself that it isn't happening. Many sexually abused children learn to cope with abuse by pretending that the abuse isn't happening or by telling themselves, "This isn't me—it's just my body. I just won't be *in* my body while it's happening."

Unfortunately, the abuse *is* happening. By not facing her problem directly, Carlene isn't able to come up with intelligent solutions to it, such as telling an adult who might make the abuse stop. Instead, she can only fantasize about "escape."

Many teenagers do run away from home in an effort to escape sexual or other types of abuse. Estimates on teenage runaways vary widely, but the National Network of Runaway and Youth Services Inc. finds that 1.5 million teens either run away or need outside care each year—usually because of abuse.

Ironically, the teenagers that run away to escape abuse often find themselves running into even more abusive situations. According to a 1984 report of the U.S. Department of Justice, some 1.5 million children under 16 are involved in pornography and prostitution. Although many of these are young children living in abusive situations, many are runaways who have chosen or have been coerced into prostitution or into work in the pornography industry.

Runaways are vulnerable to these situations because, as teenagers, they really don't have many options for earning money or much protection from abusive adults. Sexually abused children are especially prone to ending up in such sexually abusive circumstances. Perhaps that's because, due to their backgrounds, they feel that they somehow deserve to be sexually abused, or because they've been taught to confuse love and sexual abuse.

Another contributing factor may be that some prostitutes and people who model for pornography are only able to endure what they do by "tuning out" and pretending to be somewhere else. Like sexually abused children, they may pretend that they aren't really there while the prostitution is going on, or that "It's not me, it's just my body." Sexually abused children may have coped with their abuse by exactly the same means—so they are in a sense "prepared" to keep doing so.

None of this should be interpreted to mean that sexually abused teens *like* their abuse or don't really want it to end. What it does mean is that, unless they work through their feelings, they're likely to keep finding themselves in situations where they are sexually abused, one way or another. They may also be unable to enjoy positive sexual experiences, because all sexual experiences, even sex itself, seems just like the abuse—scary, repulsive, or degrading.

Marc has also chosen a common way to cope with the sexual abuse in his family. He is *promiscuous*—that is, he has lots of casual sexual relations with a wide variety of people, rather than being selective about his sexual partners.

Marc is also *acting out* sexually. That is, instead of behaving responsibly, telling a girl what she can expect from him and ending a relationship when he is done with it, Marc sets up a situation that is almost guaranteed to get the other person angry with him. By acting very sweet and attentive early in the relationship, Marc implies that he's more serious than he is. He may even believe himself that he's serious. Then, soon after, Marc allows himself to be "caught" with another girl, which naturally annoys his first girlfriend.

Marc may believe that this is all an accident. He may also believe that he's just behaving according to his instincts, that things just happen to work out the way they do. In reality, however, he is creating a situation that he isn't happy with. Marc doesn't like disappointing so many girls, and he doesn't like so many people being angry with him. He isn't really happy about not being able to get very close to any one person.

Why, then, does he act the way he does? Because Marc has tried to hide both the truth about his mother's behavior and his anger about it, he's getting his feelings about his mother mixed up with his other feelings. Marc's anger at his mother for being sexual with him is getting mixed up with his feelings about girls his own age who are sexual with him. So Marc pushes those girls away, the way he'd like to push his mother away.

If Suzy, Carlene, and Marc were able to admit that they were abused by people they trusted, they would be able to feel angry and sad about what has happened. In Carlene and Marc's cases, they might be able to take action to stop the abuse themselves or to find a supportive adult who will take such action for them. This might well be painful, but at least their feelings would be out in the open. That would make it easier for them to separate their feelings about the abuse from their feelings about other sexual experiences.

Generally, people who are abused as children find denial a very useful way of coping. If you think you can't do anything about a situation, you may well cope with it by pretending that it's not really so bad. You might literally forget that it happened, as Suzy has done, or pretend that it isn't happening, as Carlene does. Or you might make up a reason for it, the way Geneva says that her father is only trying to teach her a lesson. You might blame yourself, as Elena does, or tell yourself that you don't care, as Seth does. You might turn to something that helps you forget, the way Maria turns to food. You might even hurt yourself, the way Lou does, just to prove that it's not so bad.

When you're too young to help yourself, denial might very well be the thing that enables you to go on living long enough to grow up. But now that you're older, you do have other options. If you're physically or sexually abused, you can tell another adult about the abuse, and you can keep telling people until you find someone who believes you and acts to stop the abuse. If you're emotionally abused, you can find other adults who will believe in you and support you. In all three cases, you can begin to bring your feelings about the abuse to the surface, so that you can sort them out from your other feelings.

The catch is, you can only do these things if you're willing to admit that there is a problem going on at home and that you're not happy about it. The price you pay for this admission is that you may feel a great deal of pain—anger and grief that you've been pushing down for a long time. You may also find that parents or other family members are angry with you for not going along with them in pretending that "nothing's wrong."

The reward that you get is far greater than the pain, however. The reward is that you begin to free yourself from the effects of the abuse. If you've developed an eating disorder or a problem with drugs or alcohol, you have the chance to solve this problem. If you're having difficulties with relationships, you have the chance to overcome these difficulties. If you're endangering yourself by reckless driving or suicidal actions, you have the chance to save yourself. And, in general, you have the chance to free yourself from the feelings of guilt and worthlessness that you may have been carrying around for a long time.

It's easy to ignore the effects of abuse. And it's easy to pretend that these effects have nothing to do with physical, emotional, or sexual abuse. But only by facing the problem head-on do you have the chance of solving it. The good news is, if you face the problem, you *do* have a chance to solve it.

Here's a more complete list of the possible effects of abuse.

Physical Abuse
- Serious physical damage, possibly resulting in hospitalization, weakness, brain damage, permanent physical injury—or death.
- Damaged self-esteem, the belief that you are "worthless" or "evil."
- Desire to hurt yourself, say, by burning or cutting yourself. Sometimes this is because abused teens think they deserve to be hurt; sometimes it's because they have turned off their feelings to such an extent that they can only feel pain; sometimes it's because it's too scary to be angry at the abusive parent, so teens take out anger against themselves instead.
- Poor grades and poor work performance.
- Patterns of choosing other abusive relationships.
- Learned helplessness—the feeling that no matter what you do, you can't affect anything in your situation.
- Suicidal impulses or actions, either because teens feel they don't deserve to live, or because suicide seems the only way out of the pain.
- Substance abuse—again, either as an escape or as a suicidal impulse.
- Running away, with the further risk of being abused "on the street."
- Difficulty in forming trusting, intimate relationships.

Emotional Abuse
- Damaged self-esteem.
- Desire to hurt yourself.
- Learned helplessness.
- Substance abuse.
- Eating disorders—compulsive eating to comfort or protect yourself from painful situations; anorexia, starving yourself to disappear or to have control over *some* part of your life; bulimia, with aspects of the other two.
- Tendency to be in other emotionally abusive relationships or to become emotionally abusive.
- Difficulty in forming trusting, intimate relationships.

Sexual Abuse
- Damaged self-esteem.
- Suicidal impulses or actions.
- Eating disorders (see above, under **Emotional Abuse**).
- Sexual acting out, such as promiscuity, engaging in destructive sexual relationships, or prostitution.
- Running away, with its risks of further abuse.
- Tendency to be involved in other sexually abusive relationships.
- Difficulty enjoying other sexual relationships.
- Difficulty in forming trusting, intimate relationships.

3

Finding Solutions

So far, we've been focusing on the experience of being in an abusive relationship. This chapter focuses on how abusive relationships could be ended. In this chapter, we'll look at why people sometimes choose not to ask for help in ending an abusive relationship, why it's important to get help, and what is likely to happen if someone does decide to ask for help.

If the information in this chapter moves you to seek help for yourself or for someone you know, then go on to chapter 4 for some names, addresses, and phone numbers of places to find help. The resources in chapter 4 include hotlines where you can call and talk without giving your name.

Why People Sometimes Choose Not To Ask For Help

There are lots of reasons why people choose not to ask for help in ending an abusive relationship. Here are some of them:

- **Guilt.** Some people feel that if they are being treated badly, they must have done something to deserve it.

As we have seen, people in physically abusive relation-ships may prefer to believe that the abusing adults are acting out of love or an appropriate need to impose disci-pline. This belief may mask the pain of being abused—but it also means that the abused person feels guilty and self-blaming. This makes it difficult to ask for help or to act to end the abuse.

Emotionally abused teens have also been given negative messages about themselves by their parents. They too may have decided that their parents are right, and that they deserve the abuse they are getting.

People who are being sexually abused may have sim-ilar feelings of guilt. They may think that if they have found themselves in a sexual relationship with an adult or an older kid, they must somehow have "asked for it." They may feel especially guilty if they remember that they never said no, never physically fought back, or actually enjoyed some parts of the relationship. This guilt is fed by many of our society's attitudes about men and women. One such attitude holds that if a girl doesn't risk her life fighting off sexual advances, she must be "asking for it." Another attitude says that a boy is sup-posed to want sex all the time and should feel lucky to have sex with an older woman. These attitudes, among others, may lead some girls and boys to decide that their unhappiness with abusive relationships is really their own fault.

In all three types of abuse, the guilt may also come from being directly told by a parent or authority figure that the abused person has done something bad. In the case of physical or emotional abuse, the authority figure may have explained the abuse by saying that the child is stupid, worthless, inconsiderate, or has some other terrible fault. In the case of sexual abuse, the authority figure may have told the child that he or she "asked for it," or behaved in a seductive way.

- **Shame.** Even if physically or emotionally abused teenagers understand that they have done nothing wrong, they
  may still feel ashamed of their own inability to stop the
  abuse. In our society, boys, especially, are expected to be
  able to fight back in any situation. A boy who has been
  physically abused may feel that there's something shameful about not being able to stop his parents from beating
  him. A boy who has been emotionally abused may feel
  ashamed of being hurt by "a few harsh words."

  Likewise, in our society, girls are told, "If you act like a
  lady, you'll be treated like one." A girl who has been treated
  badly may be ashamed that she has not been able to
  somehow prevent this behavior.

  These feelings of shame may be even more powerful
  with sexual abuse. In our society, boys are stereotypically
  supposed to be tough and girls are supposed to be pure.
  So a boy who has been sexually abused may be ashamed
  to admit that he has been a "weakling." This shame may be
  especially strong if the boy has been abused by a man. No
  matter what the boy's own feelings about having sex with
  men, he is likely to be aware that many people in our
  society deride gay people. He may feel ashamed not just
  of being abused, but of having had sexual contact with a
  man.

  A girl may feel that having had sexual contact makes her
  "damaged goods" or a "loose woman." She may feel that
  others will not want to date her or marry her if they find
  out her "secret."

- **Fear of the family.** The teenager who's been abused by
  a family member has a particular set of fears. The teen may
  wonder whether other family members are aware of the
  abuse. If the abuse is known to other family members, the
  teen wonders why they haven't stopped the abuse. In
  either case, he or she may have gotten the message that
  other people in the family don't want the abuse to stop or

that they too are afraid to challenge the abusive person. In such a situation, it takes a great deal of courage to be the one to rock the boat by publicly speaking out about what's happening.

- **Fear of losing love.**   Teenagers may also feel that they'll lose the love of one or both parents if they tell the truth about an abusive parent. The nonabusive parent may even have warned or threatened the abused teen, or expressed fear that the abusing parent will be sent to jail. The abused teenager may genuinely love the abusing adult. He or she may only want the abuse to stop. Yet stopping the abuse might result in the abusive parent leaving the house, even going to jail. This may seem like a worse consequence than allowing the abuse to continue.

  This fear of losing love is especially strong in cases in which the abusive parent seems genuinely to love the child or seems to be the only person who does. In such cases, physical or emotional abuse may be followed by warm expressions of love and affection. Sexual abuse may be accompanied by love and affection, along with the unwanted sexual behavior. The teenager may not want to lose the love and affection—even if he or she would like it to be separated from the abuse.

  In other cases, the attention of the abusive parent seems to be the only alternative to neglect. The teenager may have decided that it's better to be abused then to be ignored completely.

- **Fear of threats to yourself or your family.**   Sometimes people who are physically or emotionally abusive protect themselves by making threats. The physically abusive adult may threaten to hurt the teen who reports him or her. This adult may also threaten to hurt a younger child, a parent, or a pet. The adult may actually increase his or her violence as proof that the threat will actually be carried out.

Sexually abusive adults or teenagers may also make threats. Again, they may threaten the abused person, another child or teenager, or a parent. With younger children, they may threaten pets, or they may actually kill or wound an animal to prove to the child that they are willing and able to carry out their threats. The teenager who has been threatened this way as a child will continue to be affected by it, since the abusive person has established a pattern of secrecy and fear.

In addition to the rational fear that we all have of violent threats, the abused child has an additional reason to be afraid. Because a trusted person has already acted abusively, the child has already received the message that he or she is helpless and that no one can really be trusted. A child who is sexually abused by someone outside the home may trust his or her parents enough to report the threats, depending on the messages that these parents have given, and depending on the nature of the threats. A child who is abused by someone within the home, however, may well feel that there is nowhere to turn.

- **Concern for the family.** If the family is dependent on the abusing parent's income, the abused teen may feel that to stop the abuse would be to risk the whole family's livelihood. If the abusive parent leaves or goes to jail, the family will be in serious trouble. In such a situation, the teen may feel that it's his or her job to endure the abuse, so that the abusive parent will continue to support the family financially. The teen may also fear the emotional upheaval that would result from splitting up the family.

  A similar situation arises for the children of single parents, especially single mothers. If the teen's mother seems eager to have a relationship with a man, the teen may feel that he or she is being selfish to threaten that relationship. The teen may also fear being blamed for ruining the relationship. If the teen reports the physical abuse to the authorities, or if a sympathetic adult does so, the abusive man may well be removed from the home—and the mother may blame the teenager for ending the relationship.

In the cases in which the mother has remarried, if the stepfather is sexually abusing the teenager, the situation is even more complicated. The teenager may feel that he or she knows a "secret" that will greatly upset the mother. Again, the teen may feel guilty about exposing the stepfather as a sexual abuser, since this will affect the mother's relationship with him. Again the teen may also be afraid that he or she will be the one that the mother blames, and that she will defend the man she has married.

And of course, if a single parent is the abuser, a teenager may well feel that the family depends on this person. Such a teen may feel that it's his or her "job" to endure the abuse so that the family can survive.

Why End an Abusive Relationship?

We've looked at some of the fears that keep people from stopping an abusive relationship. Now let's look at some of the consequences that might result if the relationship continues.

As we've seen, there are many different types of abuse, and everyone handles this experience in his or her own way. One common thread that seems to come up in almost all cases, however, is that abused teens find it very difficult to like themselves. In fact, you could say that many of them have decided to hate themselves.

This self-hatred stems from many of the reasons discussed above. The abused teen feels as though he or she should have been able to do something to prevent this terrible situation. Teens may blame themselves for causing the abuse to occur, or for not being able to stop it. The only explanation that teens can often find for the situation is that he or she is a worthless person who deserves to be unhappy.

Why do teenagers come up with this explanation, even though they have actually done nothing wrong? Well, it's natural for children to love their parents and to depend on them. Children likewise depend on other adults and authority figures. So it can be very frightening to imagine that a parent or another authority is the one who is acting badly. Often, it's easier for children to blame themselves. Even people who were infants when the abuse started seem to think that somehow, they should have been able to prevent it.

This feeling of worthlessness carries over into and becomes more damaging the longer the abuse is allowed to continue. People who were abused as children often marry people who treat them as badly as the abusive adult did, convinced that they deserve to be treated the same way all their lives. Women who were physically abused may marry men who beat them and, eventually, their children. Both women and men who were physically abused may batter their own children, believing it to be "normal" behavior—and, in some cases, may beat their spouses. Likewise, people who grew up with emotional abuse may repeat the pattern with their partners and children by being abused, by being abusive, or both.

As we saw with Marc, people who are sexually abused often find it difficult to trust other sexual partners. Both men and woman who were sexually abused may run through a large number of sexual partners, acting out sexually or putting themselves in dangerous situations. They may find it easy to relate sexually, but difficult to open up emotionally. Or they may seem to get emotionally and sexually close very quickly— but then be unable to sustain the relationship.

On the other hand, as we saw with Suzy, people who have been sexually abused may find it difficult to be comfortable with their own sexual feelings. They may avoid sexual relationships altogether, or seek the safety of a relationship that isn't very satisfying but seems to promise the security that they missed as children. They may feel more secure in a relationship that *doesn't* "turn them on" sexually.

In any case, people who were sexually abused as children or teenagers may grow up to marry or become involved with others who will abuse them in some way. In fact, unless the sexually abused person gets help, such a pattern is quite likely.

The consequences of abuse during childhood and teenage years frequently manifest themselves once the abused person finds employment. They continue to feel that they don't deserve to be treated well, even at work. They may accept unreasonable blame or excessive demands from employers. Or they may interpret reasonable behavior as unusually frightening, threatening, or abusive, and react with excessive fear, anger, or confusion. Survivors of abuse may find themselves in other unpleasant situations that somehow feel "natural." If parents or other authorities made them feel guilty about protecting themselves from an abusive relationship, they may grow up to feel guilty about protecting themselves from any kind of abuse.

Sometimes this carries over into an inability to make a life plan, or a difficulty with sticking to any project for very long. Teens who grew up feeling that they had no control over a key area of their life may have developed a general sense of "what's the use?" This attitude makes it difficult to approach their life with enthusiasm and energy, and leads instead to a feeling of "whatever happens, happens."

This feeling of passivity may have been a teenager's only way to cope with an abusive situation that really was out of his or her control. But if those feelings aren't worked through, the teen may feel this way even about situations that can be affected.

Occasionally, children try to protect themselves against physical or emotional pain by shutting off their feelings altogether. They figure that if feeling hurts so much, they just won't feel. Then, as they grow up, they find that they have difficulty feeling, and in showing feelings.

Sometimes these difficulties progress, becoming a lifelong pattern of depression. This sense of being weighted down, of feeling hopeless and helpless, may have its roots in an experience in which a child really *was* helpless and had nothing to look forward to for a long time. Again, if these feelings have been ignored, while the abuse was being carried on, they may carry over into other parts of a person's life and significantly outlast the period of abuse.

Frequently, teenagers who are abused try to keep their abuse a secret from teachers, friends, and, in the case of sexual abuse, other family members. This sense of carrying around a secret or living in a secret world may also have profound consequences. The teenager may come to feel deeply isolated from the rest of the world, and may continue to feel so as an adult. The feeling that "nobody understands what it's like for me" or "it's different for me than for everyone else" may make it difficult for such a person to make friends or to establish sexual relationships, even after the abuse has stopped.

Because abused children have been told lies ("Nothing unusual is happening," "I love you more than anything else in the world," "He/she didn't mean it," "It's your fault"), they may find it very difficult to trust their own perceptions of the world. After all, their own perceptions were continually contradicted by the adults whom they loved and on whom they depended.

Likewise, someone who has been abused may have difficulty in correctly perceiving reality. Again, that's because abused children have been systematically taught to distort their perceptions ("You can't be loved unless you let someone abuse you," "People who yell and scream at you aren't *really* angry—they're just having a bad day," "He/she isn't really drunk—only a little sick"). If this experience isn't worked through, the abused child will continue to carry around this distorted view of reality and project it onto other people and situations.

Finally, as we have seen, abused children may develop problems with substance abuse, eating disorders, or self-mutilating, reckless behavior. They may also be plagued with thoughts of suicide and may eventually feel that suicide is the only way to stop their pain.

These are all feelings that can be worked through. If the abused teen gets counseling, either as a teen or after growing up, it's possible to understand these feelings and go on to other ways of living and feeling. It's possible to change the patterns that have led to substance abuse and eating disorders; it's possible to correct a distorted view of reality and to overcome feelings of hopelessness and depression.

Working Through the Feelings

Whether or not the teenager has ever told anyone of the abuse, or taken any steps to stop it, it's still possible for that person to work through the feelings when he or she becomes an adult.

However, teenagers who are actually able to end abusive relationships while they are still going on—whether through their own actions or through those of an adult—have a distinct advantage. First, they have stopped the actual abuse from occurring and there are just that many fewer days of abuse to endure.

Second, the teen who has ended an abusive relationship—or who has named the abuser in a relationship that has already ended—has taken a very positive step for himself or herself. That teen has already taken the first step toward saying, "I am a person who does not deserve this treatment, and I know how to protect myself." This first step makes it easier to continue taking other steps, because now the teen has learned two things: 1) He or she is *not* completely helpless, not any more; 2) Some adults *can* be trusted and will support both the teen's view of reality and his or her right to be protected.

Once a person has told the truth about the abuse and begun working through the feelings, what can he or she expect? In this section, we'll talk about what you can expect from the process of working through the feelings. In the next section, we'll tell you what you might expect to happen in families, courts, and the social service system.

Working through one's feelings about abuse generally involves getting counseling or therapy of some kind. In some cases, it is possible to work through these feelings on your own, or with sympathetic friends and adults, but it is far more difficult. And in some cases the only way to work through the feelings is with some kind of trained assistance from a counselor, social worker, or therapist.

What Happens in Counseling

The first step in working through feelings in counseling is talking about those feelings. Talking about the experience of the abuse itself is also important. Particularly if the abuse has been a secret, either inside or outside the family, it's a big step simply to describe what happened.

Usually, just talking about the abuse brings up many feelings. Some of these feelings may include pain, rage, frustration, and grief or mourning, as you allow yourself to feel sad for the sad things that have happened. Other feelings may include excitement and enormous relief, as you finally have the experience of telling the truth about what happened and being believed.

One of the reasons why it's helpful to talk about these feelings and experiences with a trained counselor or therapist is that some of the feelings will be confusing. Some people feel both tremendous love and a powerful hatred for the person who abused them. Some people discover a huge amount of anger and hatred toward the abuser, and then feel frightened of having such powerful feelings. Some people find it frightening to admit that people whom they loved and depended on could hurt them so badly. Some people who were sexually abused may find it upsetting or confusing to recognize that they enjoyed some parts of the experience, even while not welcoming the abuse.

One of the things a trained counselor or therapist can help with is learning how not to blame yourself for what happened. Learning to hold the abuser responsible for his or her actions may take a long time, since often the period of self-blame will have been long. Letting go of that self-blame may be a difficult process, but it can be done, especially with help.

One of the ways that a trained counselor can help you is by giving you the chance to have another kind of experience than you had with the person who abused you. The person who abused you may have punished you for telling the truth about what happened to you—the counselor will encourage you to remember what happened accurately. The person who abused you may have encouraged you to blame yourself for what happened—the counselor will support your feeling that, as a child, you were not responsible for an adult's or teenager's actions. The person who abused you may have made inappropriate demands on you, or expected you to act like a parent—the counselor will support you in having your own feelings and in acting the age that you are. What most often seems to happen is that people who haven't worked these feelings through go on to find themselves in similar situations. Their early feelings about the world—that they are going to be abused, that they can't trust anyone—continue to be reinforced. Sometimes this is because abusive situations feel "natural," and because abused people have learned to feel guilty about protecting themselves. Sometimes an abused person will interpret a nonabusive situation as abusive or dangerous. Likewise, if you have been abused and haven't worked that experience through, you may miss some good experiences that are available to you.

The good news is that, if you do work through your old feelings and experiences, you will be able to go on to new ways of feeling and living. This is even more likely if you are able to take the positive step as early as possible during the abuse of naming your abuser and ending the abuse.

What Happens When You Tell

The first thing to remember about telling is this: Pick the adult that you think is most likely to support you in ending the abuse, and then tell that person what's going on. If you don't get the help you need from that person, tell someone else, and *keep telling until someone finally acts to end the abuse.*

It's a scary thing to finally break the silence around your abuse. You may feel that it's all you can do to tell one person. If that person reacts by blaming you, yelling at you, or failing to believe you, the disappointment may seem overwhelming.

But *don't give up.* Now that you've started to seek help, *keep going.* Accept the fact that some adults may not be much help to you and keep seeking help until you get it. The obstacles may seem huge—but the rewards are even bigger.

It's also important for you to recognize that telling someone about the abuse you face may well disrupt your family. Someone may be removed from your home or go to jail. You may be the one who is removed from the home, for a few hours, a few days, or a considerable period of time. You will not be able to control what happens once you tell; the police, the courts, and the social service system may make decisions that you don't agree with.

However upsetting the results of telling might be, the results of *not* telling are even worse. Not telling means that the abuse will continue. And no matter what the consequences, you have the right not to be abused. You have the right to live in a safe environment, with protection for your physical and mental health and physical and mental welfare. You have a right to expect the adults who care for you to be dependable and to respect you.

Even if the abuse has stopped, it is important to tell someone about it. One of the most painful effects of abuse is the sense of keeping a secret, especially a secret that seems shameful. By telling the truth about what happened to you, you'll be able to start the process of recognizing that *you* were not to blame for what happened.

Physical and Sexual Abuse

Because physical and sexual abuse are against the law, any adult whom you tell about such abuse should report it, to the social service system, and perhaps also to the police. In fact, in some states, some adults are required by law to report abuse that they know of, or even suspect. Teachers and school personnel such as nurses, counselors, and principals; doctors and other medical personnel; and social workers, counselors, and mental health workers are some of the adults who may be required to report suspected physical or sexual abuse. Of course, you yourself may also contact the social service system or the police.

In some states, a nonabusing parent who knew about abuse but didn't report it can be charged with neglect in family court. This parent may lose custody of the children temporarily or permanently.

In most states, all people who report suspected abuse are immune from prosecution if they make their report in good faith. That means that if they are genuinely concerned about possible abuse (as opposed to making up a malicious story with little or no grounds in fact), they can't be sued, even if it turns out that they were wrong. Thus the adults whom you ask to help you are not taking a great risk, legally, in helping you.

We urge you to make sure that any abuse is actually reported to someone, preferably the social service system. If the adult whom you tell simply talks to your parents, this could make you more vulnerable than before. It's important for that adult to understand that you might be punished for telling and that outside authorities must be brought into the situation to protect you.

The procedure varies in different states, but if the social service system is alerted, they will almost certainly investigate the situation. If the abuse is taking place in your home, they'll visit your home and ask to talk to the abuser. They will have the power to remove either you or the abuser from the home if they feel that it isn't safe to allow the two of you to stay there together. In some cases, particularly if there's an immediate threat of violence, the police may also be called or brought in.

If you are the person removed from your home, you may be placed with a responsible member of your extended family, such as an aunt, uncle, or grandparent, or with the family of a friend.

If such care is not available for you, you will probably be placed in foster care: that is, you'll be taken to live with another family or in a group home (with a group of other teenagers, under adult supervision), from as short a time as a couple of days to as long a time as several years. Theoretically, foster care is supposed to be short-term, but in many states, it may be used for longer periods.

The social service system and the courts may work together to order psychological treatment for you, your abuser, or both. It's possible that your abuser may learn to stop the pattern of abuse, and in that case the family may be reunited. However, such treatment is not always ordered, nor is it always possible to teach an abuser to stop the abuse. Sexual abuse is particularly difficult to treat, though it is possible in some cases.

Of course, if the abuser is not someone within your home, your family may choose to bring charges against that person for breaking the law. Possibly the judicial system will also choose to prosecute that person, regardless of your family's wishes.

It is quite often the case that many abused children are frightened of formally speaking out about the abuser because they are frightened of eventually having to face this person in court. Testifying in court can be a traumatic experience for anyone, let alone a young child or teenager, and the whole experience can be particularly frightening when the defendant is a family member. The presence of the abuser may intimidate the victim of abuse, and make the victim either "close up" or say things he or she did not mean to say.

In recent years, however, many states have enacted laws that permit victims of abuse to testify away from the accused—

in the judge's chambers, on videotape, or on closed circuit television. These methods go a considerable way toward eliminating some of the trauma of a courtroom appearance. If you are being abused, try not to let the fear of a courtroom appearance make you hesitate to come forward. Many steps have been taken and are still being devised to make the whole experience as painless as possible on all sufferers of abuse.

Emotional Abuse

The mechanisms for stopping emotional abuse are somewhat different, since this type of abuse is so difficult to prove. Therefore, it's unlikely that the social service system or court system will intervene on a teenager's behalf. However, it's still possible for teenagers to get help to cope with this type of abuse, and to take some positive steps to protect themselves from its effects.

Perhaps the best thing an emotionally abused teenager can do for himself or herself is to find other adults who can give back a different message than the abusive parent. There are adults who believe you are a valuable and worthwhile person and who will give you back that message. Finding them may take a little doing, but it will make a difference. Teachers, religious leaders, other relatives, or friends' parents may be able to offer you support.

Along those lines, you may also want to seek counseling. As we've seen, a counselor may help you work through the feelings and experience of being emotionally abused, as well as help you find resources to cope with the abuse. You may find a counselor through your school, a local mental health center, or some other community agency.

Finally, there are means of coping that you can use by yourself. You can draw on the resources of your own mind and imagination to help you combat the bad effects of emotional abuse. The following suggestions are based on our understanding that the human mind is a powerful force. Suggestions such as the following have been used by athletes and

musicians to improve their performances, as well as by prac-
titioners to treat headaches, heart disease, high blood pressure,
and other serious conditions. They can also be useful in coping
with emotional abuse.

One way of coping is to imagine a mental shield that you
can place "around your mind" when the emotional abuse
begins. Visualize this shield—what it's made of, what it's
shaped like, what color it is—and visualize this shield protecting you from the insults or criticisms that fly at you like arrows.
Practice putting this shield into place, so that you can use it to
protect yourself in abusive situations.

Of course, this "emotional shield" won't stop the abuse. But
it does help to neutralize its effects, to keep them from pene-
trating your deepest barriers and from wounding your sense
of self.

Another coping mechanism is to use affirmations. Affirmations are short, positive statements that express a positive
vision of yourself, such as "I am a valuable person" or "I
deserve to be loved and cherished." Some people like to write
their affirmations every morning and every evening as a ritual.
Others like to post affirmations in places where they'll see
them every day or several times a day, such as on their mirror
or by their bedside. Still other people prefer to memorize their
affirmations and repeat them in difficult situations.

We encourage you to make up your own affirmations, and
to use them in ways that are helpful to you. One caution
though: Keep your affirmations positive. Saying "I'm a worthwhile person" is far more useful than repeating "I'm not so
bad."

One of the most painful effects of emotional abuse is that it
sometimes seems that the critical voices are inside your own
head. When you make a mistake, your head seems to be
flooded with voices yelling "You're worthless!" or "There you
go again, jerk!" How can you cope with that?

We suggest that you learn to recognize those voices, so that
instead of being overwhelmed by them, you can respond to

them. One way to respond is simply to stop and say to yourself, "This is what I've been taught, but it isn't true. I'm not stupid and worthless; I'm valuable and worthwhile."

Another way is to remind yourself that these critical voices are only one part of you—your "critic." Another part of you is a "helper" that doesn't believe those bad things about yourself. Think of strengthening that other part of yourself, so that when the critical voices start in, you can hear your helper's voice as well. Your helper is there to remind you of the good things about yourself. Sometimes it's helpful to actually visualize a "critic" and a "helper." See if you can picture what the critic looks like, what it's wearing, what color hair and eyes and skin it has; then picture your helper as well. The purpose of this visualization is to help you gain some distance from the emotional abuse, rather than treating it as the only reality.

Of course, when you do make a mistake, it's important to acknowledge it. But mistakes are just something you *do*. The problem comes when you get that mixed up with who you are. Just because you bought the wrong kind of juice, for example, doesn't mean you are a terrible person, a failure, or someone who "can't ever do anything right."

Take Another Step

Throughout this book, we've talked about the difficulties teens have in stopping abuse, as well as stressing the importance of doing so. Without question, if you are being physically or sexually abused, the best thing to do is to take action to end the abuse. Tell an adult whom you think will believe you and act on your behalf—and if that doesn't work, keep telling other adults until you finally get results. Then be sure you get the counseling you need to cope with the experience you've been through.

That's the best you can do for yourself. But what if you're not ready to take that action? In that case, take *some* action.

Reading this book was one step. Now take another. Call an anonymous hotline and discuss your feelings with the trained counselor on the other end. If you don't give your name, there's no way that anyone else can intervene in your situation—but at least you'll have begun to get the secret out in the open.

Or talk to a sympathetic friend. You may find that just telling the secret gives you some more courage to tell an adult and demand that the abuse stop.

Keep a journal—and make sure you keep the journal in a safe, private place, to avoid further abuse if the journal is found. Tell the truth about your experience and your feelings to yourself, at least. Use the affirmations and visualization techniques described above—they can be useful for coping with some types of abuse.

Finally, remember that when you are 18, you can simply leave home. If you're being abused by someone within your home, this will end the abuse. However bad things seem to be now, they will get better, simply by the passage of time.

If you're not ready to take more direct action, then promise yourself that you will take action as soon as you *are* ready. Remember, the sooner you act, the better your chances of minimizing the effects of the abuse, both the long- and the short-term effects. In the meantime, do anything you can to give yourself another message.

If You Know Someone Who's Being Abused

If you know someone who's being abused, or whom you think is being abused, you may be wondering what you can do to help. First, ask the person about the abuse, or say something to give the person a chance to tell you about it. Abused children or teens may deny that they're being abused, but at least they've got the message that someone knows. Your message may make a difference to them later.

When you're talking to the person you think is abused, let him or her know that help *is* available and you'll help the person get it. Give the person a chance to respond to your offer. Then, if the abused person isn't willing to take action, *you* take action.

This action will differ, depending on how old the abused child is and on how much proof you have of the abuse. A child living in your home whom you know is being abused must be protected. Find the adult whom you think will most likely be supportive and responsible, and tell that adult what you suspect. If that adult doesn't respond, keep telling other adults, until you find someone who will take action.

Follow the same procedure with a young child whom you baby-sit or observe frequently if the child has told you about abuse or if you have observed the child to be frequently injured, burned, or bruised.

If you aren't sure if abuse is present, find an adult whom you trust to help you find out more about the situation.

With a teenager, your procedure will be somewhat different. A teen who is being abused has the right to make his or her own decisions about reporting the abuse. Certainly you shouldn't assume that a friend who is suddenly withdrawn or nervous, or one who is doing poorly in school, is necessarily the target of abuse. In such a situation, do what you can to find out more, to offer your support, and to let the other person know that help *is* available if he or she wants it. You may also want to talk over your feelings with an adult, in confidence, to decide further what you should do.

Imagine the Possibilities

Throughout this book, we've talked about various people, and we've seen how abuse has affected them. Now let's imagine what else might be possible for some of them.

- Geneva finally talks to a friend about her father's beatings. Her friend encourages her to tell the school counselor about it. The counselor reports Geneva's father to the social service system, and suddenly there's a court order to remove Geneva's father from the home. Geneva's mother is upset, but is relieved that the beatings have stopped. The court orders Geneva's father to get counseling before he returns home. Geneva misses her father, but she is very relieved that she no longer faces the terrible beatings. She is getting counseling at school and is beginning to feel more self-confident.

- Sixteen-year-old Lou figures he can hold out for two more years. Then one day his mother beats his little sister with an extension cord and nearly puts the girl's eye out. At the emergency room, a nurse starts asking questions. Before he knows it, Lou is telling her everything. A social worker intervenes and directs that the children be placed in a foster home. Lou misses his mother, but he realizes that he may have saved the lives of his younger brother and sister. He feels bad for his mother, but good that he was finally able to take action to protect his family and himself.

- One of Maria's teachers starts asking Maria about her home life. At first, Maria doesn't want to reveal her mother's secret. But when the teacher convinces her to go to a support group to get help with her compulsive eating, Maria agrees to go. One night, she finds herself telling the group about her situation. The group convinces Maria that she has the right to be treated like a teenager—she doesn't have to take on adult responsibilities yet. The support group leader reports the abuse, and Maria and her brothers and sisters are also placed in a foster home. Maria feels sad about her mother, but she also feels extremely relieved that she no longer has to worry about taking care of her entire family. Finally, there is someone else who can take on those responsibilities. Maria also continues to feel close to the people in her support group. In many ways, they feel like a "family" that is there for her when she needs them. Sometimes, when things go wrong, Maria still has her old feelings of being helpless and "a failure." But now she understands that these feelings come from her past experiences, that they are not the whole story, and that sooner or later, they will pass.

- Now that Jerry is 18, he knows he can legally leave home. He's had trouble doing so, especially since he lost the first few jobs he took. Then Jerry found a church program in which a group of young people go off and live in a community together, doing volunteer work. The program is a way to leave home without having to take on all the responsibilities of college or a job. Jerry's minister helps him sign up for the program and encourages him to stick with it, even when his parents object. Now Jerry is enjoying the new friends and the new experiences. He still feels timid about many things, but now he knows he can survive outside his home.

- Elena gets scared about her suicidal thoughts one night and calls a hotline. She talks for a long time with the person on the other end, and realizes that she really does feel better talking about her situation. The hotline volunteer encourages her to find a counselor, so the next day Elena calls her local mental health center and finds someone who is willing to see teenagers. Things aren't much better at home now, but Elena feels much better. She's finding friends that she can talk to about what's really going on with her, and she's joined a local teen theater group whose adult directors are very encouraging and supportive. It still hurts Elena when her mother pulls away, and she cried for a long time the night her father missed her play, but now there's something in her life besides the pain—and that's a beginning.

- Things didn't really start to change for Seth until he had been out of the house for a few years. When Seth was a junior in college, he met a woman student he really liked. He started a relationship with her, and for a while, everything seemed to be going well. Then the same old problems started cropping up: The woman told Seth that he was just too critical and too hard to get close to. Seth really didn't want to lose the relationship, and he panicked. He went to see the college counselor to talk about the relationship, and the counselor encouraged him to make the commitment to try therapy. Seth wasn't able to save the relationship he cared about, but he feels like he's finally understanding why things have been difficult for him and how they might be different. He's beginning to be more optimistic about his life, and he feels he's getting along better with both friends and the women he dates.

- For Suzy, things got worse before they got better. She had a string of bad relationships, in which she went further sexually than she really wanted to, and then was dropped by the guy just as she was getting to like him. Suzy became very discouraged and her grades started falling off. Her parents became very upset at the changes in their daughter. They went to Suzy's school for advice, and fortunately for them, the school suggested counseling for the entire family. In the counseling, the story of Suzy's early sexual abuse came out—and so did a lot of other feelings Suzy had been having about her family. Suzy's parents had to deal with the fact that Suzy was afraid to come to them about a serious problem, and Suzy had the relief of finally dealing with a painful experience. Now Suzy and her family feel much closer and much more able to be honest with each other. Suzy feels like she's finally beginning to learn that what happened with the baby-sitter wasn't her fault.

- Carlene felt like she was reaching her breaking point. It was getting harder and harder to keep up the pretense that everything was okay. One day Carlene saw a TV movie about a girl whose uncle was sexually abusing her. Carlene began to realize that maybe her situation wasn't unique. In the movie the girl finally reported the problem. Carlene realized that she could tell her secret, too. She chose to talk to her grandmother. Her grandmother didn't want to believe that such a thing was possible. She told Carlene that if Carlene behaved herself, the stepfather would, too. Carlene realized she had to tell someone else. After a week or so, she talked to a teacher, although it was difficult for her to do so, and she started and stopped many times before she actually told. The teacher reported the abuse to the social service system right away. The social service system got a court order to keep the stepfather out of Carlene's home. Carlene's mother was very angry with Carlene, but Carlene was experiencing a whole new sense of relief that the sexual abuse had stopped. Carlene and her mother were ordered to get counseling, separately and together. Gradually, they're beginning to talk about what happened. Carlene, too, is beginning to understand that what happened wasn't her fault.

- Marc's story was a lot like Seth's. For several years, he managed to continue in the same pattern. Then he found a woman he really cared about and realized how tired he was of going from relationship to relationship. The woman liked Marc a lot, but insisted that he needed to get counseling if their relationship was going to work. They started going to counseling together, and Marc realized again how much he wanted to change his patterns so that he could make a different choice. He began seeing a counselor by himself. So far, he doesn't notice much difference, but at least he's managed to stay in this relationship longer than any of the others; and he's optimistic that things may work out.

As you can see, there are no guaranteed happy endings when it comes to abuse—but things can definitely get better. If you are being abused, or if you know someone who is, we urge you to take advantage of the resources in the next chapter. Taking steps to end an abusive relationship is never easy. But it may be the beginning of a whole new chapter in your life.

4

Where to Find Help

The following organizations are involved with issues of child abuse—its prevention and treatment.

A1-Anon Family Group Headquarters
One Park Avenue
New York, NY 10016
212-302-7240
See the white pages in your telephone book for the group in your area. Al-Anon helps those over the age of 13 deal with problems created by alcohol in their families.

American Humane Association
63 Inverness Drive East
Englewood, CO 80112
303-792-9900
The American Humane Association protects children against neglect and abuse through a variety of community service programs.

Big Brothers-Big Sisters of America
230 North 13th Street
Philadelphia, PA 19107
215-567-7000

Big Brothers-Big Sisters provides a broad range of programs for children and teenagers, including matching children from one-parent homes with adult volunteers.

Barbara Sinatra Children's Center at Eisenhower
  Medical Center
39000 Bob Hope Drive
Rancho Mirage, CA 92270
619-340-2336
This is an outpatient therapy center for children who have been physically and sexually abused.

Boys Town, U.S.A.
Communications and Public Service Division
Boys Town, NE 68101
402-498-1111
This is a national organization for troubled boys, girls, and families and has several programs dealing with residential care, short-term shelter, and family preservation.

Child Abuse Listening Mediation, Inc. (CALM)
P.O. Box 90754
Santa Barbara, CA 93190-0754
805-965-2376
CALM works for the prevention and treatment of child abuse through family therapy and community education programs.

Childhelp USA
6463 Independence Avenue
Woodland Hills, CA 91370
1-800-4-A-CHILD
Childhelp provides crisis counseling information and referrals in situations dealing with child abuse.

Children's Institute International
711 South New Hampshire Avenue
Los Angeles, CA 90005
213-385-5100
Offers group counseling, individual counseling, family therapy, and a referral service.

Clearinghouse on Child Abuse and Neglect Information
  (a division of The National Center on Child Abuse and
  Neglect/Children's Bureau-NCCAN)
P.O. Box 1182
Washington, DC 20013
703-821-2086
Provides information and referrals through a DIALOG database.

Kempe National Center for the Prevention and Treatment
  of Child Abuse and Neglect
1205 Oneida Street
Denver, CO 80220
303-321-3963
This organization provides individual and group therapy for children who have been victims of child abuse. It also provides consultations to professionals who work with children and families.

National Center for Missing and Exploited Children
2101 Wilson Blvd. Suite 550
Arlington, VA 22201
703-235-3900
"America's resource center for child protection."

National Committee for Prevention of Child Abuse
332 South Michigan Avenue, Suite 1600
Chicago, IL 60604
312-663-3520

This organization provides education and referral programs on child abuse to the public.

National Council of Jewish Women
53 West 23rd Street
New York, NY 10010
212-645-4048
Provides information and referrals.

National Council of Juvenile and Family Court Judges
University of Nevada
Box 8970
Reno, NV 89507
702-784-6012
This institution has a continuing education faculty that provides courses and training for judges who handle juvenile sexual abuse cases.

National Network of Runaway and Youth Services, Inc.
1400 I Street NW., Suite 330
Washington, DC 20005
202-783-7949
This national organization is divided into regional networks and provides services and support for families and youth at risk for child abuse, drug abuse, AIDS, or alcoholism.

Parents Anonymous
520 S. Lafayette Park Place
Suite 316
Los Angeles, CA 90057
213-388-6685
PA has free self-help support groups for parents who are under stress and want to learn healthy ways of parenting. It also offers free support groups for their children.

SCAN (Suspected Child Abuse and Neglect)
902 High Street
Little Rock, AR 72217
501-372-7226
This private organization investigates and works one-on-one
with families of children 13 years old and younger who have
been physically, emotionally, and sexually abused.

Society for the Prevention of Cruelty to Children
161 William Street
New York, NY 10003
212-233-5500
To report a child now being abused, call: 1-800-342-3720
This organization provides referrals and counseling to families
and children suffering from physical and sexual abuse.

National Runaway Switchboard
1-800-621-4000
This organization provides referrals for runaway children.

INDEX

101